2100 Laughs
For All
Occasions

Also by Robert Orben

THE JOKE-TELLER'S HANDBOOK

THE AD-LIBBER'S HANDBOOK

THE ENCYCLOPEDIA OF ONE-LINER COMEDY

2500 JOKES TO START 'EM LAUGHING

ORBEN'S CURRENT COMEDY
(a topical humor service for public speakers)

2100 Laughs
For All
Occasions

Robert Orben

DOUBLEDAY & COMPANY, INC.
GARDEN CITY, NEW YORK

Library of Congress Cataloging in Publication Data

Orben, Robert.
    2100 laughs for all occasions.

    1. Public speaking–Handbooks, manuals, etc.
    2. American wit and humor.   I. Title.   II. Title:
    Twenty-one hundred laughs for all occasions.
    PN4193.I50734   1983   818'.5402
    ISBN 0-385-23488-0 (pbk.)   AACR2
    Library of Congress Catalog Card Number 82-45448

INTRODUCTION

There is more order, precision and method in the creation of jokes than most people realize. And so the challenge of "making a funny" has engaged some of the great minds of history.

Did you know that Leonardo da Vinci, for a brief period in his life, was a stand-up comic who wrote and performed his own material? As described in *The World of Leonardo* by Robert Wallace and the Editors of Time-Life Books, Leonardo played the lute, sang and recited satires and jests at the court of Ludovico Sforza in Milan. Take my paintbrush, please!

Centuries later, another extraordinarily inventive mind became fascinated by jokes. Thomas Alva Edison filled hundreds of notebooks with the results of his experiments—but a few of his notebooks were filled with jokes. He used them to maintain morale and as a shot of comic adrenalin for his overworked staff.

What is there about humor that appealed to both Leonardo da Vinci and Thomas Alva Edison? My answer would be the almost mathematical precision of jokes. Comedians may seem to be free spirits—clowns may epitomize chaos—but what they say and do is as disciplined and structured as any Marine Corps drill team. Humorists may break the rules of society, decorum and taste, but never the rules of comedy.

What would a course called Funny 101 teach? To create a joke you have to pick and choose from seven ingredients:

1. SUBJECT MATTER—the background history of what or whom you're going to needle.
2. KEY ELEMENTS—the cliché words, phrases and joke points associated with the subject.
3. FUNNY SOUNDS AND CURRENT SLANG—K is funny (Kankakee). S is funny (Sufferin' Sassafras).
4. ATTITUDE—are you for it or agin it?
5. AUDIENCE ATTITUDE—are your listeners for or agin it?
6. COMEDY FORMULAS—exaggeration, understatement, wordplay, an abrupt change of thought, etc.
7. COMEDY CONSTRUCTIONS—the framework of the joke; good news, bad news—how cold was it?—etc.

By mixing and matching, these seven factors provide trillions of comedic possibilities—and, from Leonardo to Woody Allen, every comedy writer has followed this route. Indeed, in time, there is no doubt in my mind that computers can and will be programmed to write jokes. Just program the seven inputs, press the MIX & MATCH key, and watch the kneeslappers pour out.

But humor-users need not be humor-creators. In fact, much of today's humor is acquired humor. The laughmaker extracts from books, publications, services and observation the one-liners and stories that fit his or her personality and position. In time, a reservoir of instant and apt comedy response can be developed and drawn from as needed.

Think how many times you've been asked the same questions about your background or job. For example, I'm frequently asked for my middle name. My answer is: "I don't have one. I came from a very poor family." It comes across as an ad-lib—and many years ago, on one occasion, it was. But effective ad-libs are not to be flung and forgotten. Add them to your comedic memory bank.

For the more frequent user of humor, a working personal gag-file should be considered. Whenever you discover a joke or a story that's right for you, transcribe it onto a 3 × 5 or 4 × 6 index card. Then duplicate and cross-index this card under all possible uses and subject classifications. To illustrate, here's a joke from an issue of my humor service, ORBEN'S CURRENT COMEDY: "When I was twenty, I prayed for a million dollars. When I was thirty, I prayed for a million dollars. When I was forty, I prayed for a million dollars. Now I'm fifty and I've come to two conclusions: either I'm praying for the wrong thing—or God isn't picking up His messages."

I would make up five identical cards listing this joke to be filed under AMBITION, MONEY, PRAYER, RETIREMENT DINNER and RECOGNITION EVENT. Additional classifications that reflect your specific needs may be added. As the file grows in size and scope, it should answer most of your humor requirements.

In addition to preparing for specific occasions, read through the gag-file now and then to keep the material fresh in your memory. In time, the comedy constructions and formulas that make the jokes work will become part of your unconscious. And, given enough time, you will become your own joke computer.

But what has all this to do with business? Where do jokes figure into job descriptions? How does wit mix with widgets?

Well, let's take another look at those two famous laugh-getters we met up front. Leonardo da Vinci and Thomas Alva Edison demonstrate many of the uses business humor can be put to.

Leonardo as a stand-up comic had to put his audience at ease and then effectively communicate with them. Every member of today's business community faces this same challenge. That first minute or two in front of an audience is critical. The right relevant opening joke can bond an audience to a speaker, ease tension and melt resistance.

EXAMPLE: I once gave a speech on the third day of a convention that was held during a heat wave in July. The hotel air conditioning was either not working or not up to its task. For three days it was Swelter City. My personal problem was that I was talking to a group of people passionately devoted to a subject I knew very little about. So I began by pointing out just how intimidated I was to be speaking to an audience so jam-packed with experts and authorities in the field. "And as a result," I added, "I'm standing up here with all the confidence and self-assurance of the man who runs the air conditioning in this hotel."

Suddenly the audience and I were as one—hot, uncomfortable, and with a common enemy. Laughter. Applause. I gave the rest of my speech, not to an audience, but to friends.

Humor communicates in other useful ways. In prehistoric times, mankind often had only two choices in crisis situations: fight or flee. In modern times, humor offers us a third alternative: fight or flee—or laugh.

Laughter is an ideal tension breaker. An apt joke gives everybody involved enough time to draw back, rethink a position or reconsider an action. Sometimes feelings run so high on a specific subject that just a humorous reference to it is a tacit indication that the door has not been closed to further discussion. "Smile when you say that, podnuh!" is the operative thought.

Thomas Alva Edison used the humor in his notebooks as a bonding and morale-building device. He knew that people who can laugh together can work together—longer, harder and to greater effect. This concept has now led to an interesting twist in traditional testimonial and retirement dinners. Instead of rather dull programs based on maudlin recollection and syrupy sentiment, recognition events today are often in the form of roasts.

The guest of honor is gently raked over the coals in an affectionate way. And the more lofty his or her position, the more the audience reacts to a recounting of his or her foibles and failures, weak points and high points:

"This morning I had a long talk with the boss. Actually, he had a long talk. I had a long listen."

"I won't comment on the hours kept by our sales force, but they think Johnny Carson is overworked."

"I love an event like this. For thirty years a person gets in to work early and stays late every night—and when they finally retire, they're given a watch—which, if they had had one during those thirty years, they never would have come in to work early or stayed late."

But when the evening has ended, all have shared the experiences, the banter and the laughter that stings, cauterizes, heals and then unites. It is the humor of equals—the laughter of democracy. And, in business, it can add a little more balance to the balance sheet.

And now, please turn to the over 2100 jokes that follow. Add them to speeches, presentations and your everyday conversation. Use, amuse and enjoy!

Bob Orben

CONTENTS

2100 Laughs
For All
Occasions

ACKNOWLEDGMENTS

I want to thank (NAME OF CLERGYMAN) for that truly inspiring prayer, but I do have one complaint. (NAME OF CLERGYMAN), you don't know what it does to an insecure person like me to have somebody stand up before I give my speech—and pray for the audience!

ACKNOWLEDGING YOUR INTRODUCTION: I have only one thing to say: if you really believed that introduction, you wouldn't be sitting—you'd be kneeling.

ACKNOWLEDGING YOUR INTRODUCTION: I wonder if you would mind taping that introduction so I could play it back for my agent? He still thinks of me as the guy who gets 90% of *his* money.

ACKNOWLEDGING A GLOWING INTRODUCTION: Some of you may have noticed me reading during that introduction and I want you to know that it wasn't disinterest. When I heard all those wonderful things being said about the next speaker, I just wanted to look in the program to make sure it was *me!*

WHEN YOU GET A HUMOROUS NEEDLING INTRODUCTION: Hearing an introduction like that is like wearing Size 26 Jockey Shorts. You're laughing with tears in your eyes.

AFTER A NEEDLING INTRODUCTION: I don't want to start any trouble, but for those of you who are paying a baby sitter $1.50 an hour—I want you to know that introduction cost you 22¢.

WHEN YOU'RE GETTING AN AWARD: I am sure I don't deserve this, but then again, what is my opinion against millions?

WHEN YOU GET AN UNEXPECTED GIFT: I haven't been this surprised since I went to a wife-swapping party on Fire Island.

AIRLINES

I came in on _____ Airlines. God's gift to Greyhound.

They have the kind of planes that make you afraid of only one thing. It's the ground, when you come right down to it.

I only ask two things of the airline industry: for the prices to come down and the planes to stay up!

My ambition is to someday change my name to Throckmorton Wildersham Armstrong. I always wanted to fly on a monogrammed plane.

It's very easy to tell you're on a no-frills flight because, just before take-off, the stewardess comes down the aisle and asks you to fasten your Scotch Tape.

In no-frills they charge you for everything. It's the first time I ever saw an oxygen mask with a meter.

AIRPORTS

Things have really changed since the days of Christopher Columbus. Columbus headed for India and he wound up in San Salvador. Today, if you head for India, you get to India. It's your luggage that winds up in San Salvador!

They have a wonderful security system out at (LOCAL) Airport. In ten minutes, your luggage can go from matched to snatched!

Have you noticed how intimate those body searches are getting at airports? When you get through with one of those friskings, you don't know if you're in La Guardia or in love.

Have you gone through the security procedures at airports?

One guard frisked me and felt me and patted me and pressed me. He said, "Do you have any concealed weapons?" I said, "Who cares? Kiss me!"

I'll tell you how intimate the search is. One airline got five complaints. Two from passengers and three from massage parlors.

I was watching one planeload being frisked and it was fascinating. Eighty-seven passengers were in transit and one old maid was in heaven!

You ought to see this old maid. It's amazing. She's been three days out at the airport getting frisked. What makes it so amazing—she doesn't even have a ticket!

And I'm getting a little suspicious of my wife. This big, tall, handsome guard frisked her and said, "We must do this again sometime." She said, "How about now?"

People are worried about mid-air collisions and I don't blame them. Yesterday two airliners were so close together, the flight controller had to throw cold water on them.

Traffic is so heavy over every major airport, flight controllers are using a new technique. Every time a plane takes off, they yell, "Fore!"

I won't say how many close calls there have been but if you're a stewardess the first thing you learn how to say is, "Coffee, tea or YIPES!"

And as every air traveler knows there is sort of an unwritten law about swerving to avoid a mid-air collision. It can only be done before the dishes are cleared—but after the coffee is served.

I've had so many drinks spilled on my lap, I get fan letters from urologists.

ANNIVERSARIES

I just celebrated my Crystal Anniversary. That's fifteen years of my wife saying she can see right through me.

My neighbor recently married a woman who's active in Women's Lib, church, civic and cultural affairs. I asked him how it was working out. He said, "Fine. I just celebrated our Paper Anniversary." I said, "Paper Anniversary?" He said, "That's one year of coming home and finding a note saying my supper is in the refrigerator."

APARTMENTS

The walls in our apartment are so thin, yesterday I called up the landlord and said, "You've got to do something about our neighbor's TV set." He said, "You can hear it?" I said, "I can see it!"

I don't want to complain about this building, but the elevators should only go up as fast as the rent.

I was looking at apartments in one of those high-rise buildings where the rent increases $5.00 for each floor you go up. I swear, I don't see how God affords it!

I don't want to complain about our building but, like the President, we're surrounded by Secret Service men. These service men are so secret, the only time you see them is at Christmas.

BABIES

The government is worried because the birth rate has fallen below the replacement rate. Don't worry. Just put more men on the job!

We know a couple who have eight kids and they practice birth control. The reason they practice it—they're obviously not very good at it.

I make it a point never to lie to my kids. This morning one of them came up to me and asked, "Where do little babies come from?" And I gave him a straight answer: "Sheer carelessness! Sheer carelessness!"

The big problem with having a baby is getting to the hospital on time. One doctor got a phone call and a man's voice said: "Doc, she's due any minute now!" The doctor said: "Is this her first baby?" The voice said: "No, this is her husband!"

And you can always tell the difference between a first baby and the ones who come after. For your first baby you buy a $65 sterilizer and a bottle is never put in his mouth until it's boiled for two hours. Now, by the time your fifth baby comes along, it's a little different with the bottle. He's sharing it with the dog!

I love to go down to the maternity hospital and sit in the waiting room. You hear such fascinating conversations. One woman came out of the delivery room, turned to her husband and said, "Now will you believe those pills were aspirin?"

Then a nurse came out with twins and she said to the father, "I'll bet you're surprised." He said, "I certainly am." She said, "What were you expecting?" He said, "A divorce!"

The doctor told me that one day they had forty-two babies born. I said, "What do you call that? A record?" He said, "No. A company picnic!"

I always wondered why babies spent so much of their time sucking their thumbs. Then I tasted that baby food.

Be honest now. Have you ever tasted baby food? Baby food tastes like Liberace sounds!

They say there's something about having a baby that changes night into day—and that's true. It's called the Two O'Clock Feeding!

Babies are nature's way of showing people what the world looks like at two o'clock in the morning!

Did you ever get up at two o'clock in the morning to fill a bottle? I wouldn't get up at two o'clock in the morning to empty one!

I believe in taking care of myself. I was telling my doctor: "The greatest thing that ever happened to me was milk. Since drinking milk, I weigh 190 pounds!" He said: "What did you weigh before you drank milk?" I said: "Six pounds, nine ounces!"

BANK ROBBERIES

Bank robbers are so brazen these days. I saw one standing in front of a hidden camera singing: "I Want to Be in Pictures."

Isn't it amazing how many people are going around barefoot these days? About the only time you see a stocking is over a bank robber's head.

You can appreciate the mental capacity of the average bank robber when you consider that most of them can pull that stocking over their head all the way up to the toe.

I'm a very trusting person. I was in a bank today and the fella standing in front of me had a stocking over his head. I didn't know he was a bank robber. I thought he was a near-sighted podiatrist.

BANKRUPTCY

Bankruptcy is when you go from a credit rating to a credit rotting.

You can tell that business is getting worse by little things—like Bankruptcy Court putting up a sign saying: TAKE A NUMBER.

Nowadays it isn't hard to go bankrupt. All it takes is an interest in three things—wine, women and gasoline.

You know a company is in trouble when little things happen. Like, their sinking fund *is*.

Default is when a debtor says, "Notes to you!"

Things must be bad. I know a GOING OUT OF BUSINESS store that did!

They're called time payments because, if you skip one, that's what you do.

Let me put it this way: Nowadays you don't have to get a massage to be pressed for money.

I just had a frightening thing happen to me. Someone said, "I don't know how I'll ever be able to repay you." What makes it so frightening—I had just finished lending him $5000!

BANKS

I'm known as Old Bedspread at our friendly neighborhood bank. Every time I come in for a loan, they turn me down.

I deal with one of those Gettysburg Address banks. They give you little notes that are long remembered.

It's a little depressing to realize we're living in an era when banks pay more interest to you than your wife does.

You know what's wrong with the world today? Banks are guaranteeing us a ____% rate of interest until 1986—but nobody's guaranteeing us a 1986.

Frankly, I'm getting a little worried. Yesterday my neighbor ran out of cash. That may not seem so serious to you, but I live next door to a bank.

You can always tell when a bank is in trouble by little things. Like, they come around and repossess your toaster.

We have a little tradition at our house. Every Thanksgiving we invite someone who is in more trouble than we are. This year we invited the banker who holds our mortgage.

I'm very suspicious. For instance, why do banks always have six windows and only two tellers? I figure it's their way of saying it's three to one you won't get it back!

I go to a typical neighborhood bank. There are always four people standing behind the counter. One is called CLARA JONES and the rest are called NEXT WINDOW.

BARBECUES

My wife says that outdoor barbecues are a man's job. I don't mind that—but who barbecues breakfast?

We're going to an outdoor dinner.
My wife says I shouldn't be rude.
I shouldn't overeat, overdrink, overtalk—
Methinks I've been barbe-cued.

The summertime is when, if the girl next door comes over and asks you to light her fire, she's talking about a barbecue.

I made a barbecue last night and there was good news and bad news. The good news is, I had something that was done just the way I like it—pink on the inside and charred on the outside. The bad news is, it was my thumb.

Beef is now so expensive, this Saturday night we're having a little community entertainment. Six husbands standing around a cold barbecue singing: "Memories! Memories!"

BASEBALL

Our local baseball team has a pitcher who's so bad, yesterday he was 0 and 3—and this was just applying his spray deodorant!

Did you know they named a wine after the (LOSING BASEBALL TEAM)? You keep it in the cellar.

My wife likes to watch a soap opera on TV and I like to watch the ball game. You know something? With the (LOCAL TEAM), there's a lot more scoring on the soap opera.

Actually, baseball is a very simple game. It's just like driving on the freeway. The whole idea is to get home without being tagged!

BEAUTY CONTESTS

I know this sounds crazy, but the Miss America pageant has given me a goal, a purpose, a direction! If there's anything to reincarnation, I want to come back as a tape measure.

Have you noticed that they always hold these big beauty contests during a heat wave? It gives the judges an excuse for sweating.

Personally, I would never want to have a beauty contest judge as a friend. I figure, any man who can pick a girl measuring

40-26-38 because of her smile, her personality and her skill on the xylophone—will lie about other things too!

One judge was always offering encouragement to the girls. He kept patting them on the back—and some of them weren't even facing the right way.

Last Saturday my wife came home early from shopping and caught me watching a beauty contest on TV. She said, "What are you watching?" I said, "A football game." She said, "That's a beauty contest." I said, "It is? I was wondering why those shoulder pads were so low!" . . . She didn't believe it either.

BEEF

Meat is so expensive, it's ridiculous. Yesterday I brought home a three-pound sirloin steak. We didn't know whether to broil it or bronze it!

THE BIG BEEF: I think that I shall never see
A sirloin coming home with me,
To give our hungry mouths a rest
From eating chicken legs and breast.
A steak so thick and juicy red,
You hear the price and then drop dead.
A rump roast even when on sale
Is too much for a piece of tail.
I look for no one to place fault,
Just pass the pepper and the salt,
'Cause poems are made by fools like me,
But only meat prices make bankruptcy.

I just found out why they call it aged beef. You ask the price and that's what it does to you.

I get nostalgic for the good old days, when Pepsi had more bounce to the ounce—and butchers gave more chuck for the buck!

I got an invitation to a party and it said: B.Y.O.B. I called up the hostess and asked, "Bring Your Own Bottle?" She said, "No. Bring Your Own Beef!"

Beef is that red stuff you ask the price of and then order spaghetti.

BEVERLY HILLS

If you're a social climber, Beverly Hills is Switzerland.

Beverly Hills is so chic, where else do traffic lights come in decorator colors?

I once went to a Thanksgiving pageant in a Beverly Hills school. These kids reconstructed the very first Thanksgiving dinner, not from history books, but from their own personal experience—and it was fascinating. They had thirty Pilgrims, twenty-two Indians and a sommelier.

Beverly Hills is a fabulous place. This town is so rich, every Christmas they distribute baskets to people with only one pool.

There's a bank in Beverly Hills that is so exclusive—you know how some banks take a picture of bank robbers? They take an oil painting!

I love to go to a Beverly Hills supermarket. Where else can you get caviar-flavored Alpo?

I once went to a jewelry store in Beverly Hills and asked the gift counselor what I could give to my wife for $25. He said, "The sales tax."

I just don't seem to have a business instinct. For instance, last year I opened a day-old bread store in Beverly Hills.

I won't say that people in rich communities are insular, but once I bought a globe of Beverly Hills.

BIBLE

There are some who feel that on the seventh day God shouldn't have rested. He should have erased.

Do you realize if Adam and Eve hadn't eaten that apple in the Garden of Eden—a Johnny Carson suit would be Johnny Carson?

You know what would really upset this world? If an archaeological expedition went up to Mount Sinai and found one more tablet. And it said, "Disregard previous Commandments!"

I think Moses deserves a lot of credit for bringing the Ten Commandments down from Mount Sinai. You ever try to get two tablets of stone into a typewriter?

Last week I heard something that was so deep, so moving, so thoughtful—when it was over I jumped up and yelled, "Author! Author!" They threw me out. It was the Ten Commandments.

I think it helps all of us to realize that the great figures of history also had their human failings and moments of uncertainty. I prefer to think that Moses' first words on Mount Sinai were: "Who?"

Don't complain. The world could be a lot worse off than it is. What if Moses, who wrote down the Ten Commandments, had been a doctor—and nobody could read them?

My boss is very cautious. If he had been Moses on Mount Sinai, he would have gotten a second opinion.

BILLS

I'll tell you how bad things are. If you order the Businessman's Lunch, they make you pay in advance.

No wonder the post office is so overloaded. Every time I call up someone to ask for a payment, they tell me the check is in the mail!

I asked our bookkeeper how we were doing on collections. He said, "Do you really want to know?" I said, "Yes." He said, "Our PAID stamp was lost for two weeks before anybody noticed it."

It isn't worth getting upset about a customer who doesn't pay. All you can do is chalk it up to profit and louse.

Our Accounts Payable are so high, I have debt dreams.

I try to run a very honest business. For instance, this morning a delivery man brought us an electric typewriter and I paid for it with a $500 check. I said, "Are you allowed to accept a tip?" He said, "Yes, I am." I said, "Don't try to cash the check!"

We run the kind of business that pays all of its bills by the tenth—the tenth reminder.

My wife always tries to look on the positive side of things. Last night she said, "We haven't paid the butcher bill, the grocery bill, the car payment or the rent, but try to remember one thing: It is always darkest after the dawn." I said, "It is always darkest *before* the dawn." She said, "After. We haven't paid the light bill either!"

Don't be discouraged if you lose your job, have your car repossessed, look shabby because you can't afford new clothes, and always have bill collectors at your door. Something will always turn up—the noses of your neighbors.

I operate on a burnt toast budget. I just manage to scrape along.

BIRTHDAYS

Yesterday I went into a florist shop and said, "I want to send a dozen daisies to my wife for her birthday." The clerk said, "A dozen *daisies?*" I said, "Yes. I want to say it with flowers." He said, "You don't have much of a vocabulary, do you?"

For his birthday, I bought him something that's form-fitting—a tent.

I know a woman who got a divorce because of a surprise birthday party. She sneaked into her house with forty of her friends and surprised her husband—with the maid!

It was kind of interesting, what prompted my neighbor's wife to shoot him six times. He came home from work and she said, "Guess what I made you for your birthday? Bird's nest soup, oysters on the half shell, pâté de foie gras, pheasant under glass, homemade gooseberry pie, topped off by a two-dollar imported cigar and a twenty-five-year-old brandy." He shook his head and said, "Had it for lunch!"

BOSS

Bosses are made to order.

A good executive is someone who keeps up the pace of a much younger man—his assistant.

My boss has that sign on his desk: THE BUCK STOPS HERE. And it does. You can never get a raise.

When a boss says, "I gave at the office"—he's talking about a hard time.

The boss is not cheap. Let's just think of him as our designated pinchpenny.

My boss is all heart. Yesterday he turned me down for a raise and I got very emotional about it. He said, "Please. I can't stand to see a grown man cry." So he took off his glasses.

I haven't had a raise in years. In 1979, '80 and '81 money was tight—and in 1982 the boss was.

Is there anything more discouraging than telling the boss if you don't get a raise you'll have to think about moving—and he hands you the phone number of Allied?

When it comes to adult education, nothing beats contradicting the boss.

We've always had a credit crunch in our office. The boss never praises anybody.

My boss is very proud of the fact that he became General Manager of our company the hard way. He started out as President.

My boss has an instinct for making money. If I had been Thomas Alva Edison and invented the electric light bulb, he would have invented the meter.

Have you ever noticed that when the boss's son breaks the rules—the company policy lapses?

I'm a little worried about something that happened at work.

The boss always says anything goes. And this morning he started calling me Anything.

I have this unreasonable fear of getting fired. It's called Bosstraphobia.

I said to my wife, "I think the boss is trying to tell me something. This morning he said I was working my fingers to the bone." She said, "What's wrong with that?" I said, "I was scratching my head at the time!"

There are certain things that worry a boss. Like when the accounting department orders three pencils and a dozen erasers.

A boss is somebody who, when he sees red on his accountant's fingers, hopes it's blood.

BUMPER STICKERS

I just saw an interesting bumper sticker. It said: DRIVE CAREFULLY. WE NEED EVERY TAXPAYER WE CAN GET.

I just saw a wild bumper sticker. It said: HONK IF YOU LOVE QUIET!

RIP-OFF: what you do to your (LOSING CANDIDATE) bumper sticker on (DAY AFTER ELECTION DAY).

BUSINESS

I haven't done well in the business world. I once paid an outfit $10,000 to get in on the ground floor. Then I found out they were building a tunnel.

The workers in my company formed a union and want to share in what I get from the business. So I agreed. I gave one an ulcer, one a migraine, one hypertension and the rest high blood pressure.

Let's all be very grateful for the Avon lady. It's nice to know that someone in business is still ringing the bell.

You can tell that confidence is returning to the business world. Yesterday I heard a yes-man say maybe.

Did you hear about the executive who's so indecisive, they wrote a song about him? "Yes, Sir, That's My Maybe!"

Panic is that subtle emotion you feel when you realize your business has three more salesmen than customers.

I didn't realize how much business had slowed down until they put my Sunday newspaper through the mail slot.

The stores are doing so badly this year, yesterday I saw a shoplifter sneak up to a counter and leave something!

The single biggest concern of American businessmen today is the balance of payments problem. The balance of payments problem. That's when your creditors are asking for payments and you don't have any balance.

In our company, a trouble shooter would need a machine gun.

An efficiency expert and an exterminator have one thing in common: they both want to get the bugs out of your business.

A consultant is a mother-in-law with an attaché case.

If you can't say something good about somebody, talk about our competitors.

They say you profit by your mistakes. In that case, our competitors are going to have one helluva year!

I once looked into one of those franchises that say you can go into business on a shoestring. What they don't tell you is what the shoestring has to be around—$25,000!

Secretaries are devious. Mine came back from her winter vacation and said, "Would you like to see where I got sunburned?" I said, "I sure would." Showed me a picture postcard of Miami Beach!

It's always illuminating to listen to the conversations between secretaries. One said, "I'm not going out with Phillip any more. He always wants to make love in the back of his company car." Her friend said, "What's wrong with that?" She said, "He's an undertaker."

I have to admit my last company didn't do too well. It made prescription windows for nearsighted Peeping Toms.

I just met the world's dumbest businessman. A florist who closes on Mother's Day!

The main thing in life is to persist, to persevere, to always continue onward. If you give up, you will never know how close you might have been to success. Look at the inventor of Preparation G.

American ingenuity has risen to new heights. A manufacturer has just come up with a vehicle that will serve you your entire life. It's a baby carriage that converts into a wheel chair.

Good merchandising is when you offer a special on Poli-Grip and peanut brittle.

It's gotten so bad, businessmen are actually ashamed of the prices they're charging. That's right. Last Sunday I heard a garbageman praying, "Forgive us our trashprices!"

Love is in the air. Why, just yesterday I made an honest woman out of our cashier. I watched her.

I'll say one thing for our product: we have a lot of satisfied customers. The minute they bring it back, are they satisfied!

Did you hear about the public relations man who was fired? He kept treating the public like relations.

BUTCHERS

Woman was made from man's rib, which, as any butcher will tell you, isn't the best cut.

I went down to our friendly neighborhood butcher and his face was a brilliant red. I said, "Sunburn? Vacation?" He said, "Prices. Embarrassment!"

Now I know why they call them butchers. Look what they do to your budget.

I heard a butcher training a new clerk and it went something like this: "If somebody comes in and asks the price of two pork chops, you say, 'Five dollars.' Then you watch them very carefully—and if they don't wince, you say, 'And ninety-five cents.' Then you watch them even more carefully and if they still don't wince, you say, 'Each!'"

Our butcher just finished his spring cleaning. I think he started with my wallet.

For those of you who haven't gone shopping lately—a butcher does to your savings what parcel post does to your packages.

My butcher reminds me of Will Rogers. He never met a price he didn't hike.

I always wanted to be a butcher and charge $3.00 a pound for hamburger, but I don't have the proper background. My mother and father were married.

And somehow I think butchers are adding a little more fat than they used to. I just bought a pound of hamburger that had a very unusual color to it—white!

CAMPING

The balance of nature is a 42-25-36 camper with a backpack.

I know a couple who took their four kids, three dogs and two cats, and spent a one-month vacation in their camper. And it was very economical. They saved enough money to pay for the divorce.

I'll never forget our first camping trip. Believe me, there's nothing like the smell of fresh hot coffee at six o'clock in the morning. The reason there was nothing like the smell of fresh hot coffee is, we forgot the matches.

Camping is when you sleep outdoors, cook your food over a fire, wash your clothes in a bucket, and do all the things you did in the army—only now you like it!

My wife says she'll get interested in camping when you can turn a campfire down to simmer.

CAR REPAIRS

Decisions, decisions! I can't make up my mind whether to call up a mechanic and have my car overhauled or call up a junkyard and have it hauled over.

I just figured out why auto mechanics spend so much of their time lying face up on the floor. All that money can weigh you down.

My auto mechanic can never become a bank robber. There's a record of his fingerprints all over my seat covers.

People are so inconsistent. I met a fella who was very upset over the credibility gap in Washington. I asked him what he did for a living. He said: "I give estimates for auto repairs."

I don't care what anybody says, I think people are basically honest. Like this morning, I came out and the whole trunk of my car was pushed in. But under the windshield was a little note. It said: "As I am writing this, fifty people are watching me. They think I am giving you my name, address, license number and insurance company. I ain't!"

CARS

I have a great idea. Why don't we give Detroit to Canada? Then it'll be their problem!

Have you seen the latest from Detroit? It's called a stationary wagon. Never moves out of the showroom.

My brother-in-law is really resourceful. Last week he became a new-car salesman. He's still out of work but now he has a reason.

Hold everything! I have an idea that'll solve the housing crisis, increase the sales of new cars and cut down on the use of gas. It's called a three-room Buick!

Everything on a Rolls-Royce is the ultimate in luxury. You know how other cars have windshield wipers? With a Rolls-Royce you get a written guarantee from God it won't rain!

A new luxury car costs $115,000 but it'll last for a lifetime. Mostly because, when they tell you the price—you drop dead!

They have one car that's so expensive, you don't wash it. You dry-clean it!

People just don't think. Do you realize what it costs motorists each year to add oil to their cars? Why don't they just get longer dipsticks?

To the man who stole my car while it was twenty degrees below zero this morning, I have only one thing to say: "Keep the car. Just tell me how you got it started!"

If you want to improve your gas mileage, do what millions of other car owners do—lie!

I once bought a used car with 286,000 miles on it. It was owned by a little old lady from Pasadena—with grandchildren in Tibet!

CARS (SMALL)

I bought one of those little cars that get 34 miles to a gallon. There's only one problem. You have to put it in low to get off a piece of gum.

I love those little cars because they're so intelligently arranged. One of them even has a place just big enough to hold your keys, a pack of Kleenex and some maps. It's called the trunk.

The nice part about a subcompact car is, it can still go from 0 to 60 in ten seconds—only now it's feet.

If you want to drive up to the mountains, you don't put it in low. You put it in the garage and take a bus.

CHEAPNESS

We're living in a time of open-heart surgery and closed-heart giving.

Cheap? Who puts out a tableful of potato chips, pretzels, potato salad, cheese dip, crackers, cake, cookies and candy—and uses a scale as a centerpiece?

Cheap? His idea of being forced to commit an unnatural act is picking up the check.

Cheap? Who do you know has a wind-up pacemaker?

Cheap? He had his name legally changed to Bernard Victor Dillingham, just so he could have monogrammed shorts.

CHILDREN

There's one big difference between whiskey and kids. Whiskey improves with age.

Don't let this get around but I've come up with something that could revolutionize the field of child psychology. It's called a whip!

Let's face it. Some kids are like ketchup bottles. You have to hit them to get them moving.

Personally, I have never raised a finger against one of my children. I use the whole hand—it works a lot better.

I always wanted to spend more time with my kids. Then one day I did.

A typical American home is where you tell your dog to "Speak!" and your kids to "Shut up!"

I take a very practical view of raising kids. I put a sign in each of their rooms: CHECKOUT TIME IS 18 YEARS.

My kids complain so much, I have a new sign for our home: BELLY ACRES!

I think the only word this kid has ever been at a loss for is "Good-by!"

Ten years old is such a wonderful age. It's when you still don't know that having a girl friend is a contact sport.

Kids are so diffident. Nowadays it's: BOY MEETS GIRL. BOY LOSES GIRL. BOY SHRUGS.

Words are so important. I was telling our six-year-old, "When you talk to the neighbors, just say your aunt likes to crochet. Don't call her the happy hooker!"

My kid is very conscious of presents. Last week I lost my balance and fell out of the window; staggered around to the front door; rang the bell; and she said, "What did you bring me?"

All kids need warm, sincere, enlightened reassurance. Just yesterday one of my kids came up to me and I said, "John, of course I'm concerned and interested in what you're doing. What's that? I'm sorry. David, of course I'm concerned and interested in what you're doing."

CHRISTMAS

Holidays come and holidays go,
And tempus it does fugit;
This Christmas I'm so flat-out broke—
I think that I'll just Scrooge it!

I'm beginning to worry a little about my reaction to Dickens' *A Christmas Carol.* The last few times I read it I came away with the strong impression that Marley's ghost had a big mouth.

Here it is Christmas and it seems like just yesterday the kids came home from camp. It was just yesterday. We kept refusing them.

Isn't it amazing how early stores put up their Christmas decorations? Here it is November 29th and there are more Christmas trees covered with dust than tinsel!

Christmas is such an exciting time. Kids are asking for toys and games and bikes and Santa Claus is going, "Ho! Ho! Ho!" And fathers are looking at the price tags and saying, "How? How? How?"

Before Christmas, I like to curl up at night with a good book. My checkbook. It's the only way I can keep my wife from using it!

Christmas is when your bank account is seasonally adjusted.

I'll never forget Christmas in my home town. We could never afford that big red Santa Claus outfit, so we used the next best thing—a nudist with high blood pressure.

Every year millions of American husbands and wives gather up their kids and go out to Grandmother's house for Christmas dinner—because there's something about it they can't resist. The price.

Every year for the last fifteen years we've been going out to Grandmother's house for Christmas dinner, and when we leave, she always takes my hands in hers and calls me a voluntary longshoreman. And only this morning I realized what a voluntary longshoreman is—a free loader.

I know a newlywed who got a terrible shock on Christmas Day. She found something in her stockings—her husband.

If you live in an apartment, it's getting harder and harder to celebrate a traditional Christmas. You ever try to hang up your stockings over a hibachi?

City kids have a difficult time understanding the Christmas story. When I said that Mary and Joseph had to spend the night in a stable, my daughter asked, "What's a stable?" I said, "Picture your room without the stereo!"

The good news is that, in honor of Christmas, the city is finally going to do something about the condition of its streets. It's going to deck the holes with boughs of holly.

The week after Christmas is always a very exciting time. For instance, if you work at the Complaint Desk of a department store, it's just like being pregnant. The pains come two minutes apart.

I believe in planning ahead. In January I bought 200 half-price Christmas cards. Last week I addressed them, put stamps on and stashed them away in a safe place. Next February I'll still be looking for that safe place.

CHRISTMAS (OFFICE PARTIES)

Office parties come and go,
A seasonal endeavor.
But the rings the drinks leave on your desk
Go on and on forever!

If Christmas is a gift from heaven, I think office parties come from the other place!

I won't say what goes on at some of these office parties but I think they're trying to put the X back into Christmas.

You can always tell the old hands at Christmas office parties. They're the ones who apologize on the way in.

The boss is shrewd. No doubt about it. Do you know how he cut down on food expenses at the Christmas office party? He had the receptionist eat pickles and ice cream and six salesmen lost their appetite.

Have you noticed how Christmas office parties always turn into football games? The men become quarterbacks and the women turn into pass receivers.

I got my face slapped at the Christmas office party. I guess there are some things you just don't ask for by their generic name.

I heard a very smooth approach at an office party last night. This fella brought a girl a drink and he said, "Here it is—scotch with a chaser." She said, "Where's the chaser?" He said, "Speaking!"

It is easy to tell who is insecure,
You don't have to be a smarty;
Just look who jumps up to answer the phone
At the annual office party.

Our firm has sort of a traditional Christmas office party. Our biggest customer is the Lang Manufacturing Company, and if their elderly president, Mordecai Lang, gives us an order in January, we're set for the rest of the year. So every Christmas our entire staff rises to its feet and with tears in our eyes we sing: "Old Lang Sign!"

We had a wild office party last year. One of the secretaries wore a skirt that was thirty-two inches from the floor. What made it so wild, she's a midget!

And you hear such fascinating bits of conversation at office parties. Like: "Where's the bookkeeper?"

"Didn't you hear? The boss accused him of stealing."
"Did he leave in a huff?"
"No. A Rolls-Royce."

CHRISTMAS PRESENTS

Christmastime is here and the air is filled with the sounds of sleigh bells, children's laughter and packages marked FRAGILE dropping down chutes at the post office.

Perfume is always popular at Christmastime. This year they even have perfumes for men. One is called SAY WHEN. SAY WHEN! Then there's a perfume for husbands who have been married twenty years—SAY IF!

I was telling my neighbor that last year my wife got real burned up at my Christmas present to her. She claimed the color was right but the size was all wrong. He said, "What did you give her?" I said, "A five-dollar bill."

If you think it's cold now, wait'll your wife sees what she didn't get for Christmas.

Can my brother-in-law eat? For Christmas I'm giving him a battery-operated fork!

There are all kinds of ways of finding yourself on the unemployment line. Like telling your boss you wanted to send him a card thanking him for your Christmas bonus—but that would have used it up.

We know a bachelor who had a terrible Christmas. He got a belt, some socks and a new girl friend—and they're all three sizes too large!

They say the human body is 92% water. All I want for Christmas is Dolly Parton and a straw!

They have some wild presents this year. How about the gift for the drunk who has everything? A Bourbon Pik!

They really have some weird gifts this Christmas. Like for $300 you can buy a remote-control fire hydrant. It's for people who always wanted to see a hydrant sprinkle a dog.

Whoever said, "Talk is cheap," never listened to a kid tell what he wants for Christmas.

When it comes to getting toys, most kids have the same philosophy: if at first you don't succeed, cry, cry again!

My kid was a little disappointed in what he got for Christmas. Actually, he was a lot disappointed in what he got for Christmas. He even asked if Santa Claus had malpractice insurance.

I gave my kid a book for Christmas and he didn't know what to do with it. There's no place to put batteries.

Batteries are very important at Christmastime. They're what make things work. I'm giving a dozen to my brother-in-law.

Everything is so commercial. With each succeeding Christmas I get the feeling that what we're really celebrating is the birth of discounting.

CHRISTMAS (SANTA CLAUS)

At Christmastime there are many names given to the one who brings gifts to all the peoples of the world: Santa Claus, St. Nicholas, Kris Kringle, Father Christmas, the United States Government.

Santa Claus goes around the entire world in one night. He delights the children; inspires the adults; and infuriates the post office.

I dig Santa Claus. You don't know how rare it is to meet someone on the give.

Santa Claus is the fella who lands on the roof, comes down the chimney, and it's called Christmas. In our neighborhood, it's called prudent.

My kids are always curious how Santa Claus can get into our apartment when we don't have a fireplace. I just tell them he comes in through a hole in Daddy's pocket.

Nowadays I get very depressed playing Santa Claus. I'll tell you what it is. Thirty years ago, if I wanted to look like Santa Claus, I had to put a big pillow in front of me. Now I just have to loosen my belt!

I'm getting a little suspicious of my brother-in-law. He's the only department-store Santa Claus I know who takes December off.

One department-store Santa Claus showed up drunk, which was awkward enough. But what really made it embarrassing, the first little girl he talked to went back to her mother and said, "Guess what? Santa uses the same mouthwash as Daddy!"

These two kids were talking and one said, "Do you believe in Santa Claus?" The other kid said, "Naah! Santa Claus is just like the Devil. It's your father!"

One store is so busy, it has two Santa Clauses. One's a speed Santa for kids who want only ten toys or less. . . . That'll be the day!

I'm so broke, if I hung up my stockings for Christmas, Santa Claus could fill them from either end!

It used to be that Christmas was when Santa Claus came

down the chimney. Now it's when your savings go down the drain!

One department store is really crowded with parents bringing their kids to see Santa Claus. So I edged a little closer to Santa and found out why. When the kid finishes his long list of things he wants for Christmas, Santa just smiles benignly, pats him on the head and says, "Forget it!"

Frankly, I didn't realize how tight things were until I talked to Santa Claus on the phone. We chatted a bit. Then I said, "By the way, how's Rudolph?" He said, "Delicious!"

CHRISTMAS TREES

But it's nice to know that youth still has a feeling for Christmas. I visited one of the dormitories at (LOCAL COLLEGE) and I saw something there that brought a tear to my eye—a marijuana plant with tinsel.

Remember when if you stayed up half of Christmas Eve assembling something—it was a bike instead of a tree?

They say only God can make a tree. I believe it. Who else could understand those instuctions?

Be honest now. Did you ever figure to see the day when Christmas trees came in decorator colors?

People don't care if a tree clashes with the Christmas spirit. Just so long as it doesn't clash with the drapes.

We've always been unlucky with those plastic trees. Our guests think it's artificial and our dog thinks it's real.

You can't believe how emotional this little dog gets about that tree. All I can tell you is, it brings tears to our floor.

I love trimming Christmas trees. First you put on the star—followed by the lights, followed by the ornaments, followed by the candy canes, followed by the tinsel, followed by February!

I wonder if God has ever looked at a tree with tinsel on it and said, "This is an improvement?"

This year we're having a very practical Christmas tree. Instead of lights we're hanging bills from the electric company.

All over America people are putting ornaments on Christmas trees. There's even a name for them—the Happy Hookers!

I just went down to our friendly neighborhood Christmas tree lot. Christmas trees are what they sell. A lot is what they get.

Maybe I'm just sentimental, but every year there's something about a Christmas tree that brings tears to my eyes—the price!

I won't say what they're getting for Christmas trees, but if you buy one, it doesn't mean you have money. It means you had money.

Things change. I can remember when Christmas trees grew wild. Now you ask the price and *you* grow wild!

Every Christmas I have this terrible decision to make. Whether to pay my son's tuition at Harvard—or buy a six-foot tree.

I got a holiday bonus of $250 and it really came in handy. I used it as a down payment on a Christmas tree.

Buying a Christmas tree can be a shock. You should see what they offered me for $50. Looked like a spruce with arthritis!

This tree was so puny, it came with orthopedic tinsel!

There is such a thing as justice in this world. Yesterday I saw a TV repairman complaining about the price of a Christmas tree. . . . He said, "Seventy-five dollars? That's ridiculous. How can you possibly justify charging seventy-five dollars for a tree?" The guy in the lot didn't bat an eyelash. He said, "Because it takes ten years to get the vertical right!"

I paid $75 for a Christmas tree but it'll serve a twofold purpose. Up until Christmas dinner I'll use it as a tree. And after, as a toothpick.

It's ridiculous. I paid $75 for a tree that looks like Mickey Rooney with tinsel.

I paid $75 for a tree that's so small, I had to kneel down to put on the star!

That tree is so small, I don't know whether to put it in my living room or my buttonhole!

Be honest now. Don't you feel a little silly paying $75 for a Christmas tree? You've been trimmed more than the tree is.

You know something is wrong when you pay $75 for a tree and you bring it home in your car—and you own a Volkswagen.

I can remember when the biggest problem with buying a Christmas tree was: "Will it fit in your living room?" Now it's: "Will it fit in your budget?"

One of those fellas who sell Christmas trees in empty lots had a serious accident last night. He fell off his wallet.

CHURCH

Gentle persuasion is when you take the felt out of the collection plates and ask for a silent offering.

A church never has to worry about the members who clasp

their hands during the prayer. It's the members who clasp their hands during the collection.

Protect us from members who, when it comes to giving, stop at nothing.

CITIES

The city just hired a consumer affairs expert, which is just great. I've always wanted to have an affair with a consumer.

Traffic in this town is so bad, they now have three crossing signs: WALK, DON'T WALK and GOTCHA!

My secretary says that riding the subway during the rush hour is a religious experience. It starts with the laying on of hands.

Have you noticed the streets in this town? I stepped into a pothole that was so deep, I didn't know whether to yell "Oops!" or "Geronimo!"

The problem with this town is, nobody wants to get involved. We have the world's only Olympic team for shrugging.

CLOSINGS

I see that my time is up and so I will end with the most effective closing a speaker can have—his mouth.

The sound of laughter and applause is food and drink to a performer. Thank you for not putting me on a diet.

(LOOK AT YOUR WATCH) I'm going to stop now because I only have three minutes left of my allotted speaking time—and I usually need that for applause.

And now, if you'll excuse me, Christmas is almost here and there's one more thing I'd like to wrap up—this speech.

In closing, let me leave you with this bit of holiday advice: Never stand under a partridge in a pear tree—'cause more than the Christmas spirit may be upon you!

Before I close, I've been asked to make this announcement: (READ FROM A SLIP OF PAPER) Will the owner of a blue 1973 Buick with the license plate UQ 1840, please report to the parking lot. Your headlights are on. I dunno. Can you imagine the idiot who's in so much of a hurry, he can't even remember to turn off his car lights? Boy, is that dumb! (LOOK AT THE PAPER AGAIN) UQ 1840. (REACH INTO YOUR POCKET AND PULL OUT YOUR CAR KEYS. LOOK AT THEM A MOMENT, THEN LOOK BACK AT THE PAPER. LOOK UP AND SAY): Thank you and good night. (HOLD UP YOUR FINGER AS IF TRYING TO GET SOMEONE'S ATTENTION OFFSTAGE AND HURRY OFF)

CLOTHING

I like Southern California because of the weather. It's just great. Where else can you buy a seersucker overcoat?

I like that outfit. I didn't know Fruit of the Loom made tuxedos.

I went into a clothing store—the salesman showed me one suit for $400. He said it was made from virgin wool. I said, "That's nice, but I'd rather see something for $100 from a sheep who fooled around a little!"

Isn't that ridiculous? Virgin wool? Of course it's virgin wool! How many sheep can afford a motel?

Isn't this a lovely tuxedo? A hundred per cent virgin wool! I know it's 100% virgin wool. The legs keep crossing.

You can always tell a rented tuxedo at an affair. It's in style and the owner isn't.

There is a very easy, practical and enjoyable way of making your old double-breasted suits into single-breasted suits. Overeat!

One thing about paternity suits—they never go out of style.

For feeling pain that's really a pipper,
Try being careless when closing your zipper!

Salespeople are so rude these days. I went into a haberdashery to buy a tie and the salesman held up one for $20. I said, "Could you show me something cheaper?" So he held up a tie for $10. I said, "Could you show me something cheaper?" So he held up a tie for $5.00. I said, "You don't understand. I'd like to see something *real* cheap." So he held up a mirror.

One day my brother-in-law took me to his tailor and it was an experience I'll never forget. It's the first time I ever saw a pushcart with a fitting room.

If you ask kids why they look so sloppy, they say they do it to be a part of their peer group. When I was a kid, I didn't even know what a peer group was. I thought a peer group was people with weak kidneys.

When it comes to dress, my kids are quite moderate. They're halfway between Brooks Brothers and Ringling.

I won't say my daughter is sloppy but I'm trying to convince her that the latest fashion is a see-through room.

The dumbest thing I ever heard is training bras. Tell me, what are you gonna teach them?

My wife and I went to a fashion show and we saw a model wearing a see-through bathing suit. And my wife got very upset. She said, "It's shameful. Why, if I looked like that, I wouldn't even leave our room!" I said, "You know something? If you looked like that—neither would I!"

And these fashions really give you a whole new look. Last Saturday night we were going out, so my wife put on her five-inch heels, a blond wig, blue eye shadow, false eyelashes, silver lipstick. Then she went into the kids' room and said, "Now drink your milk, go to bed at nine, and I don't want to hear from the baby sitter that you caused any trouble!" Blew them a kiss and left. One kid turned to the other and said, "Who was that?"

My wife bought a new Easter outfit. I think it's an Easter outfit. It's too early for Halloween!

My wife has the greatest pair of support stockings ever made. These stockings are so great, she had to get a run in them just to sit down.

I'm getting a little suspicious of our friendly neighborhood druggist. He has a new sign saying: PANTY HOSE—$1.98. INSTALLED—75¢.

We've come a long way from the days when, if a hemline was raised, so were eyebrows.

My wife refuses to wear pants suits. She says nobody is going to pull the wool over her legs!

Pat is a terrible name for a woman. For instance, she can never wear it on the front of a sweater.

It's so cold in our apartment, my wife goes around wearing a body stocking, a slip, a blouse, a vest, a sweater, a jacket and a coat. When I get romantic, it's like peeling an artichoke!

COFFEE

They say that coffee keeps a lot of people up. With me it's *Playboy*.

Did you ever stop to wonder about people who sit around for hours drinking instant coffee?

They now say that coffee can cause heart attacks. Only if the machine runs out!

I never realized how much of a stimulant coffee is until last week, when a friend of mine who drank fifteen cups of coffee a day dropped dead. And three days later he was still mingling at the funeral!

He was so charged up—you know how they usually take the dear departed out to the cemetery in the back of a hearse? He sat up front with the driver!

As they were lowering him into the ground, the minister said, "Does anyone have any last words?" And from the coffin came, "Heavy on the sugar!"

COFFEE HOUSES

I went to one of those sophisticated, chichi-type coffee houses. They're called chichi 'cause you take one look at the prices and sheee! . . . Three dollars for coffee but you get your choice of three different types of cups—small, medium and clean.

My agent keeps booking me into coffee houses, which is frightening. Do you know what it's like to do an act like this in front of an audience that's wide awake?

Performing in a coffee house gives you a false sense of security. After their third cup of coffee, you don't know whether you're hearing applause or hearts pounding.

Coffee houses are a totally different experience. For instance, in a night club people who overindulge burp. In a coffee house they perk!

You can always tell a coffee-house regular by three things: they have high blood pressure, a rapid pulse and brown teeth!

That's the mark of a coffee-house habitué—brown teeth. They look like a test pilot for Hershey!

And you'd be surprised how many romances start between one coffee-house regular and another coffee-house regular. It figures. Who else could stand that breath?

COLDS

I hate to get a cold because I have a very tender nose. You think I'm kidding? Who else do you know has an orthopedic handkerchief?

Sometimes I get the feeling the only thing that really works within the system is cold germs.

They say feed a cold and starve a fever. I have only one question. How could Orson Welles have that many colds?

One of the most frightening words ever spoken is *"Gesundheit!"* To you, no. To a diamond cutter, yes!

COLD WEATHER

I'll tell you how cold it is. Yesterday four people were playing strip poker—for keeps!

It's so cold up in San Francisco, six people bought ear muffs. Five kids and a topless waitress!

One day it got so cold, you know that picture of Adam and Eve down at the art museum? Adam was wearing a thermal leaf!

I just found out why they call it the whooping crane. It's from sitting on cold nests.

There are only three ways to be warm and comfortable on a day like this: put on heavy woolen clothing; drink lots of hot steaming liquids; and just as you're about to open the door to go out—don't!

I just heard the dumbest thing. Someone in Minneapolis, Minnesota, singing, "Won't You Come Home, Bill Bailey?" And Bill's in Miami.

At this time of year, it's so cold in Nome, Alaska—they have a marble statue to the Unknown Exhibitionist. Well, it isn't exactly marble. And it isn't exactly a statue. What it is is the Unknown Exhibitionist.

They say M & Ms don't melt in your hand. Big deal! In my apartment, neither do ice cubes!

This cold weather is causing a lot of misunderstandings. Like, if a girl says she wants to slip into something more comfortable—she could mean Florida.

I'll tell you how cold it is. Last night somebody gave me a hotfoot and I said, "Bless you!"

COLLEGE

I'm a little worried about my daughter in college. She's majoring in astrophysics, nuclear computation, biochemistry and candle making. . . . And she's failing one of them. . . . Astrophysics. Don't get ahead of me like that.

A college that gives athletic scholarships can make up the expense in other ways. For instance, their Department of Primitive Anthropology doesn't have to take field trips. It can just look at the football team.

For all you parents who are trying to figure out the sex of the weekend guests your kids bring home from college—it's easy. Put HIS and HERS towels in the bathroom. Then go in and feel which is wet.

A new report claims that 59% of college coeds are no longer virgins. They must be those undergraduates you keep hearing about.

I don't know what goes on in those dormitories but yesterday a kid graduated magna cum lewder.

It's amazing how many kids are going to college who don't know how to read or write. It's ridiculous. I know one kid who flunked registration.

Did you ever get the feeling the only tests college kids are taking is blood?

Some people go to college for an education; some for the athletic program; some for the social life. All I ever wanted to get out of college was me.

June is when college graduates take their diplomas in hand and go out to conquer the world. July is when the world counterattacks!

COLLEGE TUITION

Have you noticed what's happened to college tuition fees? Now I know why they're called Back to School sales. If your kids want to go back to school—sell them!

A lot of schools today are PASS-FAIL. If you've got the tuition, you can't fail to pass.

It's only a question of time before they print the diploma on the back of the receipt.

COMMITTEE

The best way to learn how to do it yourself is to criticize the way the committee is doing it.

In committee work, be wise, beware, man;
Miss one meeting and they elect you chairman!

If you want to kill time, a committee meeting is the ideal weapon.

COMPUTERS

Maybe machines are taking over the world. This morning I found a sign on our computer. It says: TO ERR IS HUMAN.

Every day the modern businessman is faced with new and unique problems. We just had to let our senior programmer go. Tell me, how do you get a computer in trouble?

CONCEIT

Conceited? He thinks they wrote a song about him: "The Best Things in Life Are Me."

Conceited? He could gain five pounds just from swallowing his pride.

Conceited? His idea of being unfaithful is turning away from the mirror.

Conceited? He has the only head in town with stretch marks.

CONTEMPORARY LIFE

This is a rough world we're living in. Nowadays you gotta be pretty brave just to be a coward!

In every field you really have to be tough to survive these days. For instance, they now have the Salvation Marines.

Yesterday I met my first Gay Lib cop. I mean, I don't mind being frisked—but for jaywalking?

Motorcycles are very popular today but have you ever spent eight hours on one? It's like being circumcised the hard way.

If you really want to get depressed, look at an average day's mail and then consider how many letters are worth the postage.

It's very important to work twelve hours a day, seven days a week, and never take any vacations. How else are you going to finance your heart attack?

Things really haven't changed much in the last few hundred years. Miles Standish got John Alden to speak his love. We get Hallmark.

I heard a fascinating conversation between a customer and a clerk in a greeting card shop. It went something like this:
"How much is the card that says YOUR LOVE IS WORTH THE WORLD AND ALL ITS TREASURES?"
"Twenty-five cents."
"Do you have something cheaper?"

The Gross National Product of the United States is now three trillion dollars. Four trillion dollars if you include garage sales.

A garage sale is when your neighbors clean out your attic.

A Girl Scout sold me some cookies,
With a fervor that knew no bounds.
She gained herself a merit badge,
I gained myself five pounds!

Nice guys finish last. So do people who read the instructions.

We're really living in confused times. You can tell. This morning a Four Way Cold Tablet asked me for directions.

Last week I got a massive shot of Vitamin C and a massive shot of Vitamin E—and it's just fantastic. I keep getting this terrible urge to go up to strange women and whisper, "You wanna cure a cold?"

Dear Dr. Pauling: I have been taking 50 Vitamin C pills a day and I haven't had a cold in three years. There's only one problem. I keep rolling out of bed.

It's beginning to look like the only place where the customer is always right is in courtrooms.

I think it's just amazing that the Book-of-the-Month Club has done as well as it has. I mean—they don't even have a pool!

What this world really needs is a reverse Xerox machine. You put a piece of paper in—and it disappears!

Adult education is for people who are thick and tired of it.

I have an idea that could bridge the generation gap. It's called a martini malted.

Nirvana is having a house, a car and your sinus free and clear.

CONVENTIONS

The only problem with conventions is, sometimes the participants get carried away with dreams of romance. For instance, I was down in the restaurant, and I heard the girl at the door saying: "Sir, (OR NAME OF POPULAR CONVENTION ATTENDEE), you're all confused. I'm the hostess. The only thing I put out is the menu!"

It was one of those conventions where after every cocktail hour they played "The Star-Spangled Banner"—to see who could still stand up.

Let us keep in mind that old saying: An ounce of convention is worth a pound of sales letters.

Incidentally, our efficiency expert is attending this convention.

In fact, he's down in the lobby right now—making up foursomes to go through the revolving door.

I don't know why they keep referring to the "conventional wisdom." At most conventions there's very little.

COOKING

Adam and Eve in the Garden of Eden ate fruits, nuts and berries and they called it Paradise. So would my wife. No cooking.

My wife is very big for cookouts. Whenever I ask her to cook, she says, "Out!"

I want to thank the chef for that very interesting meal. Now I know why we all prayed before we sat down to eat it.

Is nothing sacred? I just saw a supermarket display of one of those instant foods you just have to heat up in an oven—and the sign said: APPLE PIES—LIKE MOTHER USED TO FAKE.

I can understand burning steaks. I can understand burning chops. I can understand burning roasts. But Jell-O?

I always get suspicious of any cookbook that tells me to take heaping tablespoons of water.

CRIME

There is one thing you can count on in those old Westerns they show on TV. The good guy always wears a white hat. And you really get to believe this. Last week I was held up by a guy wearing a white hat and I didn't have any money. I wrote him a check!

The first thing you notice about the guy who comes around to collect for a loan shark is—he's big. I mean, how often do you see someone wearing bar bells as cuff links?

When it comes to efficiency, you just can't beat the Godfather. Who else sends out GET WELL cards two days before they're needed?

You overhear the most fascinating conversations in elevators. Like:
"Did you hear that Little Louie just spit in the Godfather's eye?"
"Little Louie just spit in the Godfather's eye? I'd sure like to shake his hand."

"You can't. There's a lily in it."

It's wonderful to live in a progressive city. I understand we're now going to have Speed Courts. They're for crooks with eight crimes or less.

Crime prevention in this town is a cop-out. If you don't believe it, run into any police station and ask for a cop. And they'll say, "Out!"

Remember the good old days, when crime in high places was somebody getting mugged in the Empire State Building?

Have you noticed how everybody seems to be running these days? Either you're a jogger trying to keep your figure or a citizen trying to keep your wallet.

According to the police, if you hold your purse by the strap and under your arm, nothing will ever happen to you. Unless your name happens to be Bruce.

They say this city is only tenth in the national crime ratings. So why do I always run back from a walk?

The crime problem is when people in all walks of life—run.

How times have changed. I can remember when an empty car with the hood up meant HELP! Now it means HELP YOURSELF!

Crime has finally reached the richer suburbs and it's a great leveler. Never before have so many of the stuck-up been stuck up.

I won't say how frightened people are but when was the last time you saw anybody buy prune juice?

You can't imagine the things that are happening in this town. Yesterday somebody hijacked a garbage truck! Called up City Hall and said, "Send $5000 or else you'll never see this garbage again!" You think that's dumb? They paid it!

I just saw a classified ad in a New York newspaper that says it all. It read: FOR SALE—BURGLAR ALARM, THREE LOCKS, AND STEREO TAPE OF A VICIOUS BARKING DOG. MOVING TO ARIZONA.

Have you been following the big trial? My feeling about one of the witnesses is that if we were walking down the street together and we met Truth—I'd have to introduce them.

Have you noticed how everybody shows up with statements and notebooks and logs and diaries? I distrust people who are that organized. I mean, I'll believe any witness whose wife sits behind him with her hair up in curlers.

DAUGHTERS

Would you believe it, my eight-year-old daughter is suffering from the heartbreak of psoriasis? It was the first word on her spelling test.

You have to feel sorry for kids who wear braces. My daughter has so much metal in her mouth, when we want her for dinner, we don't call her. We just hold up a magnet.

My daughter was a Girl Scout for six years, selling cookies. Then she was an Avon lady for six years, selling toiletries. Last week we had to take her to a doctor to have something removed from her hand—an ingrown order book!

My daughter said she couldn't live without a hair dryer, so I got her one—a chair near the oven.

If you really want to upset your daughter when she graduates from high school, give her something that'll provide her with transportation when she goes to college—a bus token.

It's an incredible experience when your daughter finally gets married, moves out, and you go into her room for the first time in fifteen years. We had to clean the rug with a lawn-mower.

I'll tell you what my daughter's room is like. When she comes out, we ask her to wipe her feet. . . . We don't want her tracking up the world.

I'm her father and I wouldn't go into her room without two things—an invitation and a tetanus shot!

I won't say what her room looks like, but it's the first time I ever saw a roach running with one leg over its eyes.

I always used to admire the pepper-and-salt rug she had in her room until one of the peppers started moving.

DENTIST

Orthodonture is the dental technique that keeps children braced and parents strapped!

I never even knew what an orthodontist was until I sent my kid to one. In three years he straightened out *his* teeth and flattened out *my* savings!

The first thing you learn from an orthodontist is that buck-teeth is the condition—not the price.

I was watching one of those old Dracula movies on television and every time Dracula kissed a girl he drew blood. I think my kids go to the same orthodontist.

I think my dentist is in trouble. Last week he took out all my gold fillings and put in I.O.U.s.

You know what I love about dentists? They tell you to open your mouth wide; they shove in a tube, a mirror and a clamp —then they say: "Now tell me what's wrong!"

I believe in preventive dentistry. Any time my dentist wants to drill, I prevent him!

I don't wanna say anything about my dentist but, on Halloween, you're looking at the only fella who bobs for applesauce!

DIETS

Most of us live lives of diet desperation.

You know what amazes me? How many young people today are on diets. When I was a kid it was easy to go on a diet. Just show up for dinner two minutes late!

You remember those days. Some of the meals were so small, I used to burp from memory!

Two groups of people are preoccupied with the Last Supper—clergymen and dieters.

CHOCOLATE LAYER CAKE DIED FOR YOUR THINS!

The doctor gave my wife a 900-calorie-a-day diet and said, "Follow this schedule religiously." And she did. She took one look at it and said, "My God!"

Before I went on my six-week fast, I couldn't touch my toes. Now I can touch my toes. I fall down a lot.

After a while you get obsessed with the idea of eating. For instance, we're sitting here comfortably with our drumsticks crossed, but what we really have our minds on is food.

Crazy things happen during this time of the year. This morning I saw a woman running down the street. I said, "Jogging? Exercise?" She said, "No. Water diet. Emergency!"

Now there's a big controversy about the low carbohydrate diet. On the low carbohydrate diet you can eat all the steaks, chops, roasts, eggs and bacon you want and it's guaranteed to keep you slim—particularly around the wallet.

But you can never give up the low carbohydrate diet. One of those skinny, slender, slinky models was on it for a year. Ate bacon, eggs, heavy cream, steaks dripping with butter, pork chops—never gained an ounce. Then one day she ate a piece of candy. What can I tell you? They had to cut her out of the living room!

The low carbohydrate diet is fantastic. I know a fella who gave up carbohydrates and went down from 288 pounds to 114. What makes it so fantastic—this included the coffin.

Dieters have the same problem as Dracula's victims. It's that first bite they have to watch out for.

I haven't had a good square meal in so long, I just enrolled for a course: REMEDIAL BURPING!

Do you know what it's like eating cold cuts three times a day? I don't get heartburn—heartcool!

I wish they wouldn't keep talking about biting the bullet. I mean, what kind of a diet is that—bullets? I even need bicarbonate after oatmeal!

I'm on such a strict diet, I can't even listen to dinner music.

Bikes are great for losing weight. Last week I bought a racing bike and just like that I lost ten pounds. Not riding it—assembling it.

I'll say one thing for my wife's relatives: they do count calories. They may need a pocket calculator to do it, but they do count calories.

You think we have troubles now? Can you imagine if worry had calories?

I had a terrible experience at a Weight Watchers' dinner. They had a sign saying: WATCH YOUR HAT AND COAT. So I watched my hat and coat and somebody stole my dessert!

There is a destiny that shapes our ends—and a lasagna that ends our shapes!

Did you hear about the diet club that went fatty dipping?

DINNERS

I like the club bulletin that didn't quite call its annual dinner a disaster. It just referred to it as a messed event.

I understand that, in China, if you burp after dinner it's a compliment. In our house it's a miracle!

Last night my wife handed me a wishbone and she said, "Make a wish." And I did. I wished there was still some meat on the bone.

DIVORCE

I'm fascinated by those real short marriages. I went to one that was over so fast, they had three figures on the wedding cake—the bride, the groom and the divorce lawyer.

My wife came up with a great idea to get a home permanent. It's called a divorce.

Alimony is like not reporting a lost credit card.

DOCTORS

The best malpractice insurance of them all is a cure.

I'm beginning to wonder about this doctor. Yesterday he rushed his first eight patients to the hospital in an ambulance. Then he found out his stethoscope was broken.

You know what bothers me? When a doctor charges you $50 to tell you you're going to have to learn to live with it. That's like a hooker telling you to take cold showers.

Whenever I go to my family doctor,
All I want from him are the facts.
Don't tell me I'm burning both ends of the candle;
I know it. Just give me more wax!

I had a terrible experience at a doctor's office today. He gave me a physical examination. Then he put on rubber gloves to shake hands.

I'm a little nervous tonight. My doctor just gave me a very unusual prescription: two aspirin and a plane ticket to Lourdes.

My doctor's the type who tries to break things to you gently. I said, "Doc, is it anything serious?" He said, "Only if you have plans for next year."

Mail delivery is so slow, it really upsets my doctor. Every time he treats a patient, the get-well cards show up after the funeral.

I'm beginning to wonder about my doctor. Yesterday I said, "What can you give me for my liver?" If I had gone to the Mayo Clinic, do you think they would have said, "A pound of onions?"

I have one of those doctors who doesn't take anything seriously. One time I went in to see him with chills and fever. I said, "What would you call this?" He said, "Do you want the technical name?" I said, "Of course I want the technical name." He said, "Shake and Bake!"

Yesterday my doctor got a fascinating phone call. This thin, high-pitched voice said, "Doc, you gotta help me. Every time I take an ocean trip, I get terribly seasick. Terribly seasick!" My doctor said, "So don't take ocean trips." The voice said, "Great! Now there's one more problem." My doctor said, "What's that?" The voice said, "I'm a herring!"

I know a surgeon who's making a fortune down in Florida. He gives nose jobs to rich alligators.

My doctor just divorced his wife and I don't blame him. Every night, just before they got into bed, she gave him an apple.

A doctor is someone who can put a stethoscope against Bo Derek's chest and hear his heart beat.

DOGS

I come from a part of the country that sets great store by manners. This area is so polite, hunting dogs don't point—they nudge.

The biggest thing in home protection today is attack dogs. They're called attack dogs because you hear how much they cost and that's what you have.

They have an attack dog for every need. They even have an attack poodle for people who steal slave bracelets.

There are now forty million dogs in this country and something's got to be done about it. We either need fewer dogs or sidewalks that flush.

We've had a little problem with our dog. It took us three months to paper train him—and another three months to convince him the paper we were referring to wasn't wallpaper.

DRINKING

They say that gasoline and alcohol don't mix. Actually gasoline and alcohol do mix. It's just that the olives get stuck in the carburetor.

They say that love makes the world go round. Only if you're that way about a brewery.

Show me a bartender in New England and I'll show you a Yankee Clipper!

I'm one of those Bigamy Drinkers. I always have one too many.

The bartender has asked me to announce that he has a special tonight. It's called a Dolly Parton cocktail. Two and you can't straighten up.

I have to be honest. I'm really not much of a drinker. In fact, the only reason I drink three quarts of beer a day is to kill the taste of the pretzels!

Incidentally, _____ won't be with us tonight. He's at the doctor's having something removed from his hand—an ingrown bottle.

My wife is still a little bugged with me. She was elected president of the Temperance Society the same day I got my head caught in a brandy snifter.

DRIVING

On behalf of all of the drivers in the audience, I want to thank the kids in the parking lot for doing a bang-up job. . . . Some people say we give our kids too much license, but I swear to you, there isn't a license among them.

Between inflation, crime, pollution and taxes—I think this pretty much sums up the way people feel: There's a sign on the corner saying DRIVE CAREFULLY. Underneath somebody has written WHY?

Be very careful on icy roads. This is the kind of weather when you can get twenty miles to a gallon even when your foot is on the brake!

I just saw the wildest identification card. It says: I AM A DRIVING INSTRUCTOR. IN CASE OF ACCIDENT—SHHHHH!

DRUNKS

Drink? This man has singlehandedly discovered a new disease —multiple cirrhosis!

My wife is still mad at me from last weekend when I came home drunk. She said, "Lips that touch liquor will never touch mine." Five minutes later she said, "What are you thinking about?" I said, "I'm trying to decide between twelve-year-old scotch and fifty-year-old lips!"

I love to come to the cocktail hour here because it's a pleasure to watch such real steady drinkers. I saw (NAME POPULAR FIGURE) out there. He's so steady he can hardly move.

It's the first time I ever saw anybody drink parcel post style. Parcel post style. He went in half bagged and came out completely smashed!

This is a very exclusive neighborhood. I once saw a wino drinking a bottle of 1959 muscatel. Well, maybe the muscatel wasn't from 1959—but the paper bag was.

DRUNK: For all you gourmets in the audience, I have a wonderful recipe for stewed clams. You open two dozen clams, put them on a plate and have him breathe on them!

DRUNK: I wish the contractor who did the walls in my house could see him. Now that's what I call plastered!

DRUNK: This may be hard to believe, but we have a lot in common. Your success is turning your head and your breath is turning mine.

DRUNK: Is it true that last New Year's Eve you took the balloon test—and it melted?

DRUNK: Sir, would you mind talking in the other direction? Your breath is melting my collar stays.

DRUNK: Sir, are you a bird watcher? The reason I ask is—I think you've had one swallow too many.

DRUNK: His wife was telling me that it's just like being married to Santa Claus. Every night he comes home with a bag on.

The best way to go through life is to be a little drunk. For instance, there was a drunk on the *Titanic*. You could tell he was drunk because he kept looking around and saying, "What a crazy way to fill the swimming pool!"

EARTHQUAKES

An earthquake is caused by two massive forces pushing against a fault. It's like your wife and mother-in-law.

Have you ever seen what a city looks like after an earthquake? It's like your son's room was contagious.

You don't know what fear is until you've sat in a San Francisco restaurant and something on your plate starts to wobble. Not Jell-O—roast beef!

I worry about things like earthquakes because I have a very sensitive stomach. Any rocking or swaying makes me nauseous. I have to take Dramamine just to look at a topless waitress.

ECOLOGY

Maybe it's time we started calling states by their ecological names. Because of roadside litter, we'll call it Messychusetts. Because of air pollution, we'll call it Phew Jersey. And because of what's happened to the Hudson River, we'll call it New yuuccck!

An ecologist is someone who writes 600-page books asking where all the trees have gone.

Most people are just not ecology-minded. I can prove it. Look at how many people got upset over the *Titanic*. Name me one person who worried about the iceberg!

ECONOMICS

I'm really amazed at the thoroughness of economic statistics. For instance, they just factored the tooth fairy into the Consumer Price Index.

I really don't know much about economics. To me, "prime interest" is when you turn to the centerfold first.

I really don't know too much about economics. To me, a liquidity problem is when the water cooler breaks.

If I understand the economists correctly, there would be no economic problem today if the poor would just spend more money.

ECONOMISTS

I'm sorry I'm a little late. I had to help an economist balance his checkbook.

I spent a quiet weekend reading the economists' forecasts for next year. I also read some non-fiction.

An economist is someone who has all the answers—but to last year's questions.

Economists disappoint you. One economist said the economy would turn up by the last quarter. Well, I'm down to mine and it hasn't.

It isn't easy to be an economist. So far they've had all the impact of a cheerleader on a computer.

Most economists have been studying the business scene for years and all this experience really helps. It lets them spot a recession the minute it's over.

ECONOMY

Remember the good old days, when we had depressions we could afford?

The government wants us to pull in our belts. They gotta be

kidding. I've already pulled in my belt so far, I've got an in-grown buckle!

They used to say if you dug down deep enough you'd reach China. Now it's the economy.

Department stores are so desperate for business, the elevator operators will let you face anywhere you want to!

We now have a beach-chair economy. You don't know what's going to fold next.

I just sent a Valentine card to the economy:

Roses are red,
Violets are blue.
I'm still here—
What happened to you?

In our house we have the Twinkies guide to the state of the economy. Prosperity is when we have Twinkies after every meal. Recession is when we have Twinkies after every other meal. And Depression is when Twinkies *is* every other meal.

Some forecasters are saying that someday we will look back on all this and laugh. How about next Tuesday?

EDUCATION

If you think education is expensive, try ignorance.

It's very hard for people without an education to make it these days. They just have to throw themselves on the mercy of the taught.

Did you ever get the feeling that kids today are getting a Teflon education? Nothing sticks!

A Ph.D. is when you drink from the fountain of knowledge and forget to say "when."

ELECTIONS

One politician has been a candidate so long he has orthopedic promises.

Is it true they're going to have express primaries for candidates with eight supporters or less?

Primaries are what separate the aspirants from the half aspirants.

This election was like a cloverleaf intersection. I've never seen so many people turning to the right.

The losers congratulating the winners have all the sincerity of a BUY AMERICAN button made in Hong Kong!

I don't have to do this for a living, you know. I have the hemlock concession at (LOSING PARTY) headquarters.

Now it can be told. Before the primaries, (LOSING CANDIDATE) was on a remote beach in New England when he picked up a sea shell, held it to his ear and a voice said, "You will be President!" Just before the nominating convention, (LOSING CANDIDATE) went up to this same remote beach in New England, held the sea shell to his ear and it said, "You will be President!" On Election Eve, after his last speech, he chartered a jet, flew all the way up to this remote beach in New England, held up the sea shell and it said, "You will be President!" Now it's the day after election and (LOSING CANDIDATE) is beside himself. He flies up to New England, goes to this remote little beach, picks up the shell and it says, "You will be President!" (LOSING CANDIDATE) says "I will be President? I lost! I lost a year of my life, thirty million dollars for my party, and I lost the election! You dumb little sea shell, do you know what this means?" And the sea shell said, "I certainly do. It's back to going (MAKE SOUNDS OF THE OCEAN ROARING)."

(ELECTION DAY) is when _____ became the Man Most Likely to Concede.

Is it true that as the election returns were forming a pattern Mrs. _____ went up to her husband and said, "_____, I've some good news and I've some bad news. First, the good news. You won't have to buy a new suit for the inaugural!"

THE ELECTORAL COLLEGE IS PASS-FAIL.

ELECTRICITY

I wish our power company would improve its insulation. I just got my electric bill and did I get a shock!

They say the electric utilities are in trouble. I didn't believe it until they sent me that wind-up light bulb.

I don't want to complain about my electric bills, but some utilities use water power, some use coal and some use oil. I think mine uses Chanel No. 5.

EMPLOYEES

The boss didn't exactly say he was inefficient. He just said he was one of the principal participants in the company's profit-shearing plan.

A good file clerk is what you have when a miscellaneous folder is what you haven't.

Our cashier wants to be in show business. She does fantastic impersonations. When she says, "Hello," she sounds just like Barbra Streisand. When she says, "Thank you," she sounds just like Phyllis Diller. And when someone forgets their change, she sounds just like Marcel Marceau.

ENERGY

This energy crisis is a lot worse than they're telling us. You know those watches that run on a single electrical energy cell? They just converted mine to coal!

Better to light one small candle than to curse the electric bill.

(TOWN WHERE BLACKOUT HAS OCCURRED) is a fun place. Where else do you need a candle to read your electric bill?

Did you ever figure to see the day when more employees would be watching the thermostat than the clock?

We're having a terrible energy crisis in our office. The boss is expecting us to show some.

It's amazing how placidly Americans have accepted the energy shortage. I never thought our motto would be: WALK SOFTLY AND CARRY A BIG CANDLESTICK!

EUROPE

Great Britain is a fascinating blend of the new and the old. Like, where else can you find a contact monocle?

I just got back from Europe and for two weeks I suffered from a very rare ailment—nymphomania of the wallet!

I'll tell you how expensive Europe is. I saw an Arab sending home for more money.

For those of you who want to spare yourselves the inconvenience of European travel, it's easy. Just drink a gallon of prune juice while looking at a picture of the Eiffel Tower by the light of a burning $100 bill.

I just got back from Europe and my neighbor asked me what it was like. I said, "I spent five thousand dollars in two weeks!" He said, "Five thousand dollars in two weeks? How did you do that?" I said, "I skipped lunches."

FALL

Here it is September—when the leaves are turning yellow and teachers aren't too confident either.

Between baseball, football, golf and tennis matches—October is the month husbands spend the greatest amount of time watching TV. In fact, one woman was concerned that, if her husband died, she didn't have anything that would remind her of the way he always looked to her. So she had a picture taken—of the back of his head.

October is when the girl you met at a summer resort and swore undying love to calls up and you respond with one word of endearment: "Who?"

FISH

Tropical fish are fascinating because you can watch them eat, swim, breed and die. Mine aren't quite so fascinating because they do it in reverse order.

I don't know why, but I always start off with an aquarium and wind up with a wet Forest Lawn.

And it's always suspicious when your kids come running in at six o'clock in the morning to tell you the fish are all floating on top of the water—'cause right away you know it isn't to get a tan!

I've always had bad luck with fish. One time we had a sick goldfish so I took him to the pet shop. I said, "What's wrong?" He said, "Rheumatism." I said, "A goldfish with rheumatism? What's the cure?" He said, "Keep him out of damp places!"

I'm beginning to wonder about this pet shop owner. One day I brought back two goldfish and I said, "I can't get them to breed." He said, "Of course not." I said, "Why 'of course not'?" He said, "Look at their fins—they're limp!"

FLORIDA

If you want to avoid colds, take Vitamin C. Take it all the way down to Florida and stay there!

It's wonderful to be in Florida during the hurricane season. Last week my car got 400 miles on a gallon.

Florida is a very romantic place to live if you're that way about alligators.

I always enjoy Florida in the summertime. You buy a steak in a supermarket and by the time you walk back home it's done.

FLOWERS

I paid $30 for a dozen roses. I didn't know the Arabs grew flowers!

I asked one florist how he could justify charging $30 for a

dozen roses. He said, "Do you know how much fertilizer goes into a dozen roses?" I said, "Not as much as went into that answer."

There's one rule in buying roses. The longer the stems, the shorter your wallet.

If flowers are the language of love, I couldn't even manage a handshake.

I'm always suspicious of people who say they came up "smelling like a rose." Is that before or after the fertilizer?

FOOTBALL

If future historians look at our TV listings for Thanksgiving Day, they could easily come to the conclusion that what we're really thankful for is football.

Women are always complaining that their husbands ignore them during the football season but that's ridiculous. Why, every weekend I make it a point to pay special attention to my beautiful blond bride. Or is it brunette?

I was watching the (LOCAL FOOTBALL TEAM)—one of the finest football aggravations in the country.

I didn't know the Super Bowl was a football game. I always thought it was a bathroom in Texas.

I don't want to say anything about the (LOSING FOOTBALL TEAM) but I've seen more scoring done in drive-in movies.

FUEL CONSERVATION

To conserve fuel, drive more slowly. As I understand it, if you drive 50 miles an hour, you use 25% less gas than if you drive

70 miles an hour. If you drive 30 miles an hour, you use 50% less gas. If you drive 10 miles an hour, you use 70% less gas. And if you're a real patriot—you back up!

I love the way they keep holding the speed limit to 55 miles an hour. Be honest now. When was the last time you saw anyone on a freeway going 55 miles an hour? In California, 55 miles an hour is for changing tires!

I read that stop-and-start driving wastes a lot of gas and that's done wonders for me. It's the first time I ever felt patriotic running a red light.

These fuel conservation measures are already causing problems. Yesterday my five-year-old came up to me crying his little eyes out. He said, "Didn't you tell me that Santa Claus goes all around the world bringing toys to good little children and he does it all in one night?" I said, "Yes." He said, "At fifty-five miles an hour?"

FUEL OIL DEALER

I've come to the conclusion that it's a lot easier to deal with the Pope than the average fuel oil dealer. With the Pope, you only have to kiss his ring.

There's a new definition of courage—giving your fuel oil dealer a bum check.

I have one of those obstetrical fuel oil dealers. Takes him nine months to make a delivery.

I just had a fantastic weekend at a winter resort. I said I was an unmarried fuel oil dealer.

FUND RAISING

A fund raiser walked into an office unannounced and found his prospect enjoying a little midafternoon dalliance with his secretary. The prospect jumped up and said, "I'm sorry. You caught me at a bad time." The fund raiser just nodded and with a kindly smile said, "For you, yes. For our Building Fund, no."

As the team captain said to the canvasser, "That was the sneakiest, trickiest, most underhanded way to get a $1000 pledge I ever saw. Keep up the good work!"

We don't refer to him as our fund raiser. Let's just say he's the chairman of the Shearing Committee.

FUNERALS

Is this man a patriot? At his funeral, they'd be afraid to play "The Star-Spangled Banner."

I got a letter this morning with good news and bad news. The good news is, my uncle spent the entire spring planting, and this week everything has started to come up. The bad news is, he's an undertaker.

Nowadays it's easy to give a patient the will to live. Tell him the price of a funeral.

Our local mortician just raised the price of a funeral. Even going down is going up.

The prices are ridiculous. Be honest now. Who needs a coffin with air conditioning?

Then again, where I'm going, maybe that's not such a bad idea.

I wish morticians wouldn't make death sound so tranquil, so peaceful, so comfortable. Everybody'll want one.

GAMBLING

I won't say he's a crook, but if you play poker with him, ask him to shuffle his sleeve.

Nevada now has five-dollar slot machines. They're for the man who has everything—but not for long!

In Nevada, money talks! And if you play a five-dollar slot machine, you know what it says? "'By now!"

All you have to do is drop in a five-dollar token and pull down the handle. I saw one couple playing and you could tell they had a little disagreement going. He was hoping he'd get lucky and she was hoping he'd get arthritis!

I met the world's unluckiest fella in Las Vegas. One night he lost $40,000 but that isn't the unlucky part. He borrowed another $40,000, went back and lost that. But that isn't the unlucky part. He went out, bought a gun, held it up to his head and pulled the trigger. But that isn't the unlucky part. The unlucky part is—he missed!

GARDENING

Gardening is best in the winter, you know. All lawns are alike under six feet of snow.

Whoever said, "What you see is what you get," never ordered from a spring seed catalog.

I was working in my garden today and the flowers looked so

bright and fresh and crisp, you'd almost think they were plastic!

Gardening is very hard work. Seeding is believing.

Gardening is a lot like X-rated movies. The first thing you have to get used to is dirt.

I was telling the fella at the next desk, "I just had the most awful experience. Yesterday our gardener poured 300 pounds of fertilizer over our garden." He said, "What's wrong with that?" I said, "It's a rock garden!"

I just spent $185 for seed, bulbs, fertilizer and tools just to plant a 20 × 30-foot garden. I swear, I don't know how nature affords it!

Have you ever planted vegetables and figured out what each one ultimately cost you? I have. Now we keep our tomatoes in a safe!

What the world really needs is a course in speed weeding!

My neighbor has the right idea. Last year he planted his entire garden with a basic ground cover—concrete!

GAS PRICES

I just bought gas for a dollar and a half a gallon. I haven't paid a dollar and a half a gallon since I bought land down in Florida.

I can remember when you turned off a highway into a filling station to get a dollar's worth of gas. Now that *takes* a dollar's worth of gas!

Gasoline is now so expensive, my wife doesn't know whether to put it in the car or behind her ears.

A customer robbed our local gas station. There's a switch!

They just raised the price of gasoline again. When you go into a filling station and they say, "Hi!"—you better believe it!

I never realized how high the price of gasoline had gone until my wife's relatives invited us over for Thanksgiving Dinner. It was cheaper than driving over here.

Remember that song "Ding, ding, ding, goes the trolley"? On a gas pump—ding, ding, ding, goes five bucks!

GAS STATIONS

Mixed emotions is hearing a gas station owner say he isn't making enough of a profit and then going into the washroom. The one with the mink roller towel.

I'll say one thing for our friendly neighborhood gas station owner: he's run short of a lot of things, but greed isn't one of them.

But it's nice to know that gas station owners haven't lost their sense of humor. I drove into one, pointed at my car and said, "Fill 'er up!" He pointed at his cash register and said, "You first!"

GAY LIB

WHEN YOU LOSE YOUR PLACE: I haven't been so confused since I tried to sit boy, girl, boy, girl at a Gay Lib dinner.

We owe a lot to Gay Lib. Thanks to Gay Lib, the opposite sex is now a multiple choice.

It was one of those gay, mad swinging weekends. The fellas were really gay and the girls were really mad.

GOLD

I just heard that gold is weakening in Europe. Sam Gold. He's on the tenth day of his honeymoon.

It really is a shame what's happened to the price of gold. I mean, this could give greed a bad name.

I can't understand why people are so fascinated by gold. You ever taste a peanut butter and gold sandwich?

It's all right to fall in love with gold, but I've never heard of a nugget kissing back.

I went out and bought a solid bar of gold but I'm a little worried about it. You know how some gold bars are stamped U. S. MINT? This one is stamped MATTEL.

GOLF

The best golfer in town is our minister. Why not? Look at all the practice he's had in keeping his head down.

My golf game and my butcher have one thing in common: they both have a slice that's cost me a fortune.

My stockbroker's a golf nut. One day he called me up and he said, "Guess what? I just broke eighty!" I said, "I know. I'm one of them."

It's easy to tell a real dedicated golfer. He can never understand how a hooker can be happy.

I think my golf game is improving. I haven't broken 100, but I'm bending the hell out of 110!

GOURMET

My wife is one of those gourmet cooks. She makes things like escargots. Have you ever taken a good look at escargots? I'll tell you something. Before I'd touch escargots, I'd eat snails!

I go to the world's worst gourmet restaurant. You know how some places serve you pheasant under glass? They serve you pheasant undercooked.

My wife is very concerned about good cooking. In fact, yesterday she spent so much time watching Julia Child, for dinner we had to send out for a pizza.

A gourmet is somebody who complains about the cheese dip at a mate-swapping party.

You could always tell the gourmets in my home town. When they order Gatorade, they always specify the year.

I really shouldn't talk about my brother-in-law because he happens to be a gourmet. He's the only one I know who puts oregano on a Big Mac.

GOVERNMENT

I think I know what Congress' problem is. Maybe they just don't want to get involved.

I dunno. Sometimes I get the feeling the government's think tank has run dry.

I can remember when America's favorite exercise was jogging up the street. Now it's running down the government.

It always bothers me when I see an elected official take the oath of office—and then wipe his fingerprints off the Bible.

One high government official is really going places. Leavenworth, that's a place, isn't it?

It isn't easy being a public figure these days. One week you're on the cover of *Time* and the next week you're doing it.

Politics is producing some wild conversations, like:
"I work for the government."
"Honestly?"
"That's my business."

Let's be fair about this—there are still a lot of honest people in government. I heard about a contractor who wanted to give a government official a sports car. The official said, "Sir, common decency and my basic sense of honor would never permit me to accept a gift like that." The contractor said, "I quite understand. Suppose we do this. I'll sell you the sports car for ten dollars." The official thought a moment and said, "In that case, I'll take two!"

In government, they very rarely fire people. They just use the subtle approach to get you to resign—like wrapping your pay check in a road map.

I like those wise old proverbs like "Half a loaf is better than none." That was first said by a city employee going out to play golf at 1 P.M.

I'll say one thing for the government. It's really keeping the prices down. Sam and Gertrude Price. This is the first year they haven't been able to fly to Europe.

GOVERNMENT SPENDING

I'll believe in economy in government when *Air Force One* is a Greyhound.

I'd have no trouble making ends meet if it wasn't for one little extravagance. I'm keeping a government on the side.

I just figured out what's wrong with the economy. We're earning money five days a week and the government is spending it seven.

We've always been suspicious of public works programs. The politicians always seem to get the money—and the public the works.

The trouble with all these social programs is, you can still call it take-home pay, but it isn't your home they're taking it to.

I think everybody should visit Washington, attend a session of Congress and see how your tax dollars are being spent. It's educational, enlightening and probably the best cure for hiccups you'll ever find.

I don't mind a _____ billion-dollar federal budget but I want to get one thing clear: does that include tips?

The proposed federal budget is _____ billion dollars. I don't know about you, but I can't even imagine such numbers. I mean, I get a headache just adding up the check at McDonald's!

A lot of people are upset by the new defense budget, but not me. Personally, I don't mind spending _____ billion dollars on guns, bombs, bullets and missiles—providing we use them in a constructive way.

It's ridiculous to spend all that money on bombs. Why can't we just get the enemy to stand close together?

GRADUATION

June is that wonderful month of achievement when millions of high school graduates have their diplomas read to them by their parents.

Graduation Day is traditionally held in June. The weather is hot. The hall is hot. The cap and gown are hot. After four years of school, it's all very symbolic. It's an introduction to sweating.

My son graduated two months ago and he still hasn't started to look for a job. This morning I told him, "I don't know quite how to put this, but when you went to that commencement—what it meant was commence!"

My kid got very upset at his commencement ceremony. The speaker said, "The world is yours!"—and he hates to be threatened.

June is when a graduate goes out to set the world on fire. July is when he starts to wonder if maybe his matches are wet.

HAIR

Nowadays you can spend $20 for an electric comb and that doesn't include the accessories. For another $9.00 you can get a power parter!

Determining a life goal is a real problem. I met one kid who has a mustache, a full beard, and hair down to his shoulder blades—and he doesn't know what to make of himself. How about a throw rug?

Gray sideburns make some men look distinguished. On me it just looks like I ran out of dye.

I know a fella who had one of those hair transplants and it was kind of touching. He bought a comb and asked if it came with instructions!

I don't wanna brag, but dark hair runs in my family. I think it's that cheap rinse!

HALLOWEEN

Life has become much more sophisticated. Years ago it was ghosts and goblins and monsters and witches that scared you on Halloween. Now it's the Dow Jones average.

I went to a recession Halloween party. There was a big tub of water and we bobbed for I.O.U.s.

I know a businessman who's great at bobbing for apples. His problem is keeping his head *above* water!

Money doesn't mean anything any more. Yesterday a mother bought her son a $39 Halloween outfit to scare his friends. The kid said, "Should I take off the price tag?" She said, "Leave it on. We'll scare your father too!"

My kid just bought a Halloween outfit—a sheet, a mask and a witch's hat. I looked at the bill. I didn't know Tiffany sold sheets.

I can remember when you went around on Halloween collecting candy and cookies and apples—and it was trick or treat. Now it's dinner.

Trick or treat is what kids play on Halloween and supermarkets play the rest of the year.

October 31st is when you play Halloween roulette. You open your door to six kids and one of them is nauseous.

I have to tell you what happened last Halloween. A five-year-old knocked on the door and my wife opened it wearing a mud pack, a chin strap, curlers and her rubber reducing pants —and the kid gave *her* candy!

HECKLERS

Sir, to have an open mind doesn't mean you also have to have an open mouth.

Pardon me, sir, but could you tell me your name? I'm on my way to Israel and I'd like to plant a weed in your honor.

My friend, bad manners are like bad teeth. Nobody knows you have them if you keep your mouth shut.

My friend, how did you ever get your lapels so wide and your mind so narrow?

Would you mind sitting down? So far you've had all the impact of an exhibitionist in a nudist camp.

Sir, NOBODY KNOWS THE TROUBLES I'VE SEEN—so would you mind getting up and introducing yourself?

I need you like a trombone player needs bursitis.

Tell me, in the pinball game of life, how does it feel to be a TILT?

You're as welcome as a hog caller in a public library.

I don't know which is wearing out faster—your welcome or my patience.

DRUNK: That's the problem with liquor. It narrows your mind and lengthens your tongue.

DRUNK: I'm not implying you've had too much to drink. Let's just say you've got a sway with words.

Sir, I don't mean to embarrass you, but if you look down, you have something open that shouldn't be. Your mouth.

Sir, if I wanted criticism, I would have stayed home. I have a wife and two teenagers.

Sir, like silicone, you're making mountains out of molehills.

Sir, I need you like the Mormon Tabernacle Choir needs bongos!

Sir, there are some things in this life that go without saying. Would you mind being one of them?

Sir, I have one thing in common with your friendly neighborhood travel agent. We'd both like to tell you where to go.

Sir, I'd ask you to speak your mind but this is no time for Marcel Marceau imitations.

Sir, I'd like to give you a Christmas present you could really use, but how do you wrap up manners?

Sir, would you mind sitting down? The Funny Suit Contest is later.

I like that suit. Didn't I see you mentioned in the New York *Times*—under the 100 SEEDIEST CASES?

Sir, you have me confused with Edgar Bergen. He was *paid* for talking to a dummy.

Sir, it's all right to give your brain to science—but shouldn't you have waited until you died?

Sir, I notice you're a pipe smoker. I have a pipe at home I'd like you to try. It's made by Con Edison.

Isn't she sweet? She has all the charm of a meter maid with a quota.

IF A HECKLER LEAVES: Sir, would you mind telling me if I said anything to offend you? I might be able to use it again.

HISTORY

I feel sorry for school kids today. Sometimes I feel that history is being made faster than they can learn it.

Who can ever forget that historic day in 1776 when Thomas Jefferson called his secretary into his office and said, "Take a Declaration!"

This is the age of equivocation. Nobody takes a stand on things. I get the feeling that if it had been written today it would have been called the Intimation of Independence!

I don't want to start any trouble—but was the Declaration of Independence notarized?

The final copy of the Declaration of Independence was made up entirely by hand. In those days, Xerox was Thomas Jefferson.

Our neighbor claims that 1776 really gave him his freedom. That was the hotel room his wife caught him in with a blonde.

Philadelphia is where Betsy Ross created the first flag. She put in blue because of the mighty oceans that beat against our shores; she put in white because of the purity of our highest aspirations; and she put in red because she cut her fingers a lot.

Actually, the Civil War was a draw. The North won it in the history books and the South won it in the novels.

You know why history has to keep repeating itself? Nobody listens!

HOLIDAYS

My brother-in-law always gets a little sentimental on these holiday occasions. As a parting toast, he raised his glass and said, "As we end this very special day, I take with me something I will never adequately be able to repay." I know. It's a $50 loan.

I'll say one thing for the Irish. They really know how to celebrate. Every St. Patrick's Day party I've ever gone to has been a regular Sodom and Begorra.

The Fourth of July is when we shoot off firecrackers, skyrockets and mouths—unfortunately, not in that order.

My wife really loves to plan ahead,
And sometimes this leads to fights.
Like, who do you know spends the Fourth of July,
Testing their Christmas lights?

Science is fantastic. Just in time for the holidays, they crossed a turkey with a porcupine. Now you can eat and pick your teeth at the same time.

HORROR MOVIES

This movie is so scary, there's a terrible traffic problem in every theater it plays. The usher shows you to your seat, looks at the screen and asks you to walk him back to the lobby.

(NAME OF MOVIE) is so frightening, the girl next to me screamed twice. Once at the picture.

I'll tell you how frightening this movie is. It's the first time I ever saw a candy stand selling Pampers.

HOSPITAL COSTS

You know what bugs me about hospitals? I'm paying $285 a day and the doctor comes in and says, "How are you feeling?" I don't say a word. For $285 a day, *he* should tell me!

I just got out of the hospital. I'm all right but my savings died.

If you go into a hospital, the first thing you have to be aware of is T.L.C. Take Lotsa Cash!

BEDSORE: what you get in hospitals when they hand you the bill.

I don't want to say anything about hospital bills, but adhesive tape isn't the only thing that's being ripped off!

This hospital was so expensive you had your choice of oxygen or Arpège.

Do you realize that hospitals charge $200 a day just for the bed? I said, "You gotta be kidding. I mean, I've paid $200 for a bed, but this one is empty!"

HOSPITALS

In case you've never seen a hospital gown, the front is rated G and the back is rated X.

It's ridiculous. You pay $400 a day for a private room, then they give you a gown that's public.

Hospitals are so crowded, they no longer have semiprivate rooms. They have semiprivate beds!

You know what's fascinating about hospitals? People in white outfits keep coming in to examine you. You don't even know if they work there!

The last time I was in a hospital, this same fella in a white outfit examined me every day. He wasn't even a doctor. He was a Good Humor man on his lunch hour!

Which explained a lot of things. I could never understand why other doctors smelled of ether and he always smelled of pistachio!

That's what gave him away. Every time a patient complained, he said, "Take two scoops of aspirin and call me in the morning!"

It's one of those hospitals where they have all kinds of code words for unpleasant things. For instance, patients never die. They just take a turn for the hearse!

People keep asking me how I feel. I'll tell you how I feel. If I saw my name in the obituary column, I'd believe it!

HOSPITAL VISITORS

I would also like to say a few words about a group of people that no hospital could do without—visitors! What makes visitors so important is: they bring the candy, fruit and ice cream that's necessary to feed the visitors who bring the flowers, books and magazines!

You think I'm kidding? When have you ever seen a patient eat anything that was brought for him? It's always the visitors. Yesterday my wife said her aunt is in the hospital. I said, "I can't go. I'm on a diet!"

And have you noticed that visitors never talk to the patient they're visiting? They spend 90% of their time talking to each other, to the other patients in the room, down the hall, even in the next ward. My wife had such a good time visiting in this hospital—I was home two weeks before she found out!

HOUSING

I get very confused about real estate terms. When the salesman showed me the house, he said, "It has a living room, kitchen, three bedrooms, two baths and den." I said, "And den what?"

We should all stand up for our rights. People who live in trailers—do the best you can.

I don't know why they say the building industry is in trouble. The poorhouse just added two new wings.

My uncle bought a house on the Mississippi River and it has everything you could possibly need—two bedrooms, a bath and an anchor.

People who spend $300,000 for a ranch house have something missing upstairs.

I live in one of those typical suburban homes. It has a picture window in front and three payments in arrears.

Remember when you could go into a public washroom, put a coin in a slot, press a button and be sprayed with toilet water? Well, this house has the same kind of fixtures.

Now I know why they call it a subdivision. Our basement is always under water.

The only thing I have saved for a rainy day is a basement that leaks.

I have a strange feeling that the house isn't too solid. I don't know why I have that feeling. Maybe it's the termites wearing crash helmets.

Maybe you know our place. It's called the House of Ill Repair.

When you get a contractor in to renovate a house, there are always subtle signs to indicate that their final bill might be a little more than their estimate. For instance, the cement mixer has white-wall tires.

I can't understand it. This house was built by a very famous name—Shacks Fifth Avenue!

But I do have to admit one thing, we have a very unusual living room—wall-to-wall carpeting. On the floor, nothing!

I haven't been the same since I decided to sell my house—so I resodded the lawn, wallpapered the living room, paneled the den, put on a new roof, finished the basement—then sold it to the one who made the best offer—the city, for slum clearance.

HOUSEWORK

I'll tell you what kind of a housekeeper my mother was. If I had brought the President of the United States home for dinner, she would have said, "Mr. President, wipe your feet, welcome to our humble home!"

My mother kept the floors of our house so clean, you could eat off them. That's right. For the first ten years of my life, I thought gravy was Johnson's Wax.

We had a rule in our house: if it didn't move, clean it! If it did move, step on it!

My mother was always cleaning something, and if you weren't careful, you were cleaning with her. In our house, cleanliness was next to Godliness—and sitting down to read the paper was next to impossible.

There's such a thing as being too much of a good house-keeper. Yesterday I couldn't take it any more. I said, "You're always cleaning and mopping and sweeping and dusting and scrubbing and waxing. It's driving me out of my mind, do you hear? Do you hear? Stop vacuuming that doorbell and listen!"

My wife is one of those housewives who spends every spare minute polishing the floors. In our house only two things are certain—death and waxes!

We have a new maid who doesn't speak much English and it makes for some exciting moments. On her first day, my wife took her through the house pointing out anything unusual. When they got to the bedroom, my wife pointed to our newest bit of furniture and said, "Water bed." The maid couldn't believe it. She said, "Water bed?" My wife nodded her head, "Water bed!" And an hour later we found the maid dutifully standing over it—with a sprinkling can.

INCOME TAX

People who don't pay their taxes in due time—do time.

Many people feel there could be a better deadline than April 15th for our taxes. How about February 31st?

When I saw what I had to come up with to pay my income tax, I was in a state of hock!

He's the kind of accountant who can put you into a fantastic tax shelter—Leavenworth.

INCOME TAX AUDITS

I had good news and bad news today. The good news is, I got a phone call and a deep, throbbing, sensuous voice said, "Your place or mine?" The bad news is, it was an auditor from the I.R.S.

Beef is high, few can afford it;
But have you ever priced an audit?

A businessman came back from an I.R.S. audit and his secretary asked him where he had been. He said, "Talking to a U.F.O." She said, "An Unidentified Flying Object?" He said, "No. An Unconvinced Federal Official!"

I made a terrible mistake the last time I went down to Internal Revenue. The auditor said, "Some of these deductions look funny." I said, "So laugh!"

INCOME TAX PREPARATION

To err is human, but this you should learn:
Don't be human on your tax return!

This is the time of year when if a person is trying to get it all together—it's receipts.

I know a fellow who had his income tax done for $25 and it really saved him a lot of money. How much can you spend in Leavenworth?

Getting your income tax done for $25 is an educational experience. The first thing you learn is that it's going to cost you more than $25.

Filling out your tax returns is like Russian roulette. You never know which blank will do you in.

INDIANS

An Indian is someone who wishes Columbus had been a farmer.

We learned a great deal from the Indians. The Indians taught us how to plant corn. The Indians taught us how to smoke tobacco. And the Indians taught us that the land belongs to all and must be cherished and preserved. Well, two out of three ain't bad.

Thanksgiving dinner began a great tradition in this country: brushing after every meal. We invited the Indians to be our guests at that first Thanksgiving dinner. Then we gave them the brush.

_____ years ago, our ancestors came to America and invited the Indians to dinner. It must have been a great dinner. The Indians are still fed up!

The Indians couldn't have had any more treaties broken if they were sent by parcel post.

Everything is relative. We claim that this country was founded in 1776. The Indians claim it was never losted.

Most talk shows remind me of a very famous Indian—Sitting Bull.

Sometimes I think my kids have part Indian blood in them. Every time I ask one of them to do something, they say, "How?"

INFLATION

The trouble with inflation is, it makes you think small. Like yesterday I found myself wondering how a canary can eat so much.

Really. We have a canary that could take the Hartz out of anyone.

You know how some canaries sing, warble and trill? He just stands there and burps!

As one interest rate said to another interest rate: "I don't know about you, but every time I look down I get dizzy!"

If you have a few minutes, think about this: inflation is when you're not doing as well as when you weren't doing as well.

There is a definite link between inflation and loss of hearing. I'll prove it to you. Every time a butcher wraps up a small steak and says, "Ten dollars," I say, "WHAT???"

Inflation is when you're afraid to go into a supermarket and ask, "What's up?"

It's the first time I ever saw a change-maker that takes fifties.

Inflation is when your pockets are full and your stomach isn't.

They call it runaway inflation but it always seems to come back.

Inflation is when, if somebody passes you a phony ten-dollar bill, it's the government.

The government keeps telling me to help fight inflation. How can I? My pay check isn't loaded!

When it comes to fighting inflation, my family are pacifists.

The inflation rate is back to ____%. I knew it the minute I dropped a dollar bill and was arrested for littering.

Inflation really has me shook up. Last night my wife said, "Take out the garbage!"—and I reached for my wallet.

Do you get the feeling the only way we're going to lick inflation is if Baskin-Robbins makes it a flavor?

You know why it's called 1983? If you paid 19 for it last year, you'll pay 83 for it this year!

Nowadays the only sure way to beat inflation is to be covered by a hedge. The one around the cemetery.

Inflation has done terrible things to this country. For the first time in history, people can't even afford to be poor.

Just think. In one generation we've gone from "We Shall Overcome" to "We Shall Overpay."

Inflation is when the price of gas goes out of sight and your car doesn't.

Do you know there's even a magazine about inflation? It's called *Payboy!*

I always wanted to get away from it all. Thanks to inflation, it's all getting away from *me!*

I sure hope they can do something about inflation. It's beginning to give work a bad name.

Just think. In one generation we've gone from saying, "Money isn't everything," to "Money isn't anything."

Inflation is when you reach into your pocket, pull out a hundred-dollar bill and say to yourself, "Good. Now I can use the exact change lane!"

Inflation has made life into one big game of golf. Even when you get to the green, you still wind up in the hole!

Nowadays there are only two things that can go from 0 to 60 in ten seconds—sports cars and cash registers.

But in spite of inflation, every night we sit down to a dinner that goes from soup to nuts. We have soup and if you expect anything more you're nuts!

Tell me, back in the thirties when you sang, "Let's have another cup of coffee, and let's have another piece of pie"—with tax and tip did you ever figure it to come to $6.73?

Inflation is when a counterfeiter buys ink, paper, a printing press—runs off $20,000,000 and loses money.

INSURANCE

Ever since I bought that $50,000 double-indemnity life insurance policy, I'm getting a little suspicious of my wife. I mean, who waxes the bottom of bathtubs?

Group insurance is nothing new. Girls used to call it a double date.

It's time we faced up to the crime problem. Either we beef up the police force or we take the life insurance machines out of airports and put them on the streets where they belong.

INTRODUCTIONS

Our next speaker is with the city. His brother doesn't work either.

Our speaker tonight is world famous. He has been written up in newspapers, magazines, trade journals, and this evening he was even mentioned on the TV weather report. They said a mass of hot air was coming up from the South.

Our next speaker has spent a lifetime boning up on his specialty and today he is one of the head men in his field. And so, without further delay, I would like to introduce one of our industry's foremost boneheads—_____!

WHEN INTRODUCING A SPEAKER WHOSE FIRST NAME IS CHARLES: And so, in the words of that grand old song, would you please CLAP HANDS, HERE COMES CHARLIE!

Tonight we present a man who stands alone—and after that cocktail hour, that isn't too easy!

When you're called upon to introduce a speaker as famous as our guest tonight, you feel a little like a bellboy in a honeymoon hotel. No matter how well you do your job, people can't wait until you leave.

Our next speaker is a man who is outstanding in his field. I hate that phrase "a man who is outstanding in his field." You don't know if he's a celebrity or a farmer.

INTRODUCTIONS (RESPONDING TO)

I want to thank you for those kind and complete remarks. As any speaker will tell you, the emcee they worry about most is the fella who claims you need no introduction and then mispronounces your name.

I'm always shook up by those emcees who describe you as "a warm human being." In Washington in August—who isn't?

AFTER A HUMOROUS INTRODUCTION: I want to thank (TOASTMASTER) for that wonderful introduction. (TOASTMASTER), I won't say how those jokes did, but if you have a life insurance policy on them—collect!

Thanks to introductions like that, our toastmaster has really made a name for himself. Unfortunately, you can't use it in mixed company.

RESPONSE TO A HUMOROUS INTRODUCTION BY A FAT TOAST-

MASTER: One more introduction like that and I'll tell Weight Watchers what you really eat.

RESPONDING TO A ROAST: I want to congratulate you on that fantastic display of terminal talent.

RESPONSE TO A NEEDLING INTRODUCTION: As the program says, this is going to be a nuts and bolts discussion of (YOUR SUBJECT). That was one of the nuts.

I.R.S.

It's very confusing to be an American. "The Star-Spangled Banner" tells us it's the land of the free—and the I.R.S. tells us it isn't.

The I.R.S. doesn't kid around. They have a new map in the lobby that shows a big eight-ball with a little X behind it and the legend: YOU ARE HERE.

I.R.S. just nailed a house of ill repute for income tax evasion. It caught them keeping a duplicate set of towels.

Ashes to ashes and dust to dust;
What stocks don't get, the I.R.S. must!

The I.R.S. works on the principle of supply and demand. What you don't supply, they demand.

What can you really say about the I.R.S.? It's like a Bermuda Triangle for money.

I still have a lot of trouble with wrong numbers. Yesterday I dialed the Red Cross and got the Internal Revenue Service by mistake. So the I.R.S. operator asked me what number I had dialed. I said, "The Red Cross—where they take your blood." She said, "Well, you aren't too far off, are you?"

You have to admire the Internal Revenue Service. Any organization that makes that much money without advertising—deserves respect!

Have you noticed that little sign in front of I.R.S.: EXACT CHANGE REQUIRED?

But it's amazing how trusting Americans are. Every year we give the Internal Revenue Service billions and billions and billions of dollars. We don't even get a receipt!

Real faith is sending Internal Revenue your return and two lottery tickets.

JANUARY

I'm glad this is January. I have only one thing to say: 19____, you won't have us to kick around anymore!

I'm really worried. It's been a week since anyone wished me a "Happy New Year." You figure they know something?

January 5th is also a very significant day. It's when you finally realize the boss isn't going to give you a Christmas bonus.

JOBS

Personnel records always ask the dumbest questions. Like: "Who to notify in case of accident?" I always put down: "A good doctor!"

My job involves a lot of little headaches all day long. It's sort of a half-aspirin way of making a living.

I don't have to do this for a living, you know. I could always go back to my old job—teaching black-eyed peas how to duck.

I have a relative who's a watchman. It's my aunt. And the man she watches is my uncle.

May is when a kid goes to a commencement exercise and is told the future is his. June is when he goes to an employment agency and is told the present is not!

I don't know what kids are always complaining about. There are plenty of jobs around. All you have to be is twenty years old with thirty years' experience.

The biggest problem a kid has is making up a résumé. When you're a kid, you can write your entire job experience on the head of a pin—and what's more, with a felt-tip pen.

My daughter has come up with a wonderfully imaginative résumé. Under Job Experience she put: Three years of professional infantile posterior placement. I think that means baby sitting.

The good news is when you say your book is in its sixth printing. The bad news is when you say your résumé is in its sixth printing.

My uncle has always had tough jobs. Take his last one—he sold venetian blinds for submarines.

The wages of sin is death! That's what I call a lousy union.

KIDS

My kid has some balanced diet. Yesterday he cut himself and bled peanut butter!

On Father's Day, I always tell my kids, "It's not the size of the gift, it's the thought that counts." And boy, do these kids think small!

Kids look on sacrifice the way the rest of us look on a lightning bolt. It's great providing it doesn't come too close to home.

When kids eat, the noise level alone will tell you why it's called "din-din."

Tell me, how can a kid complain that his pot roast is too tough to eat—and then spend the rest of the day biting his nails?

It's amazing how sophisticated kids have become. I heard two six-year-olds talking. One said, "Let's play Doctor. You operate and I'll sue!"

If we really want to do something about things that can shorten our lives—register kids!

I've never wanted to cast my bread upon the waters. My brood, yes!

"The best things in life are free." I guess that's why kids cost so much.

You have to be very careful in front of kids. Yesterday I had to explain to my five-year-old that the round thing with the bell on top is really an alarm clock—and not what I call it at six in the morning.

They say you should never swear in front of your kids. True. Then again, if you didn't have kids, what would you have to swear about?

Nowadays there's a whole new attitude. Nowadays a kid thinks he's roughing it if the school bus doesn't pull in to the curb!

It's amazing the way kids today worry. Even the little kids worry. I just saw a lollipop that comes in four different flavors —orange, lemon, lime and Excedrin!

Have you noticed how much more dynamic kids are? We used to get married and have our first baby nine months later. Today kids have cut that time in half!

Have you noticed how kids aren't too thrilled with the idea of taking baths? Yesterday my twelve-year-old came in for dinner and he said, "Is that roast beef I smell?" I said, "It is and you do!"

You've never seen a kid wear such rags. He has a pair of blue jeans. Dirty? Before we can send them to the laundry, we have to get an estimate!

That's the big thing with kids today—Vintage Grime! . . . My wife keeps saying, "Encourage him to dress better. Pat him on the back." I said, "All right. I'll pat him on the back. Where are my gloves?"

We've been having a lot of trouble with our kids and busing. The day camp keeps bringing them back.

California is a very unusual state. I mean, where else can a kid get a merit badge in weirdo?

KUNG FU

I went to an exhibition of the Chinese martial arts and it was fascinating. This fella kept lashing out with his feet, and every time he connected, he yelled, "Haaaiiiii!" I tapped him on the shoulder and said, "Kung Fu?" He said, "No. Ingrown toenail!"

You should see the way these fellas fight. (DEMONSTRATE SOME FANCY CHOPS AND KICKS.) There are only two things an expert in Kung Fu fears. Only two things—arthritis and tight shorts!

The unique part about Kung Fu is you fight with your feet.

Personally, I always fight with my feet. The minute somebody gets nasty, I run like hell!

According to Kung Fu, your feet become deadly. My kids have known this for years. They never change their socks!

LANDLORDS

Tell me, how often is a landlord supposed to paint a place? The graffiti on our walls is about Coolidge.

My wife says the landlord is a regular Devil. He couldn't be. He doesn't send up enough heat!

I'm easily confused. I always thought a home freezer was a landlord.

LAS VEGAS

I know a fella who went to Las Vegas and spent three consecutive days at the tables. Only went upstairs for a change of wallet.

Las Vegas is like Clearasil. It's guaranteed to get rid of spots— five-spots, ten-spots . . .

They're very labor conscious in Vegas. You go there and right away you join the A. F. of L. The American Federation of Losers.

I won't say what it's like to be a loser in Las Vegas, but the Welcome Wagon brings hemlock!

I don't wanna brag, but my name happens to be well known in Las Vegas. I'm the one who invented round dice. It's for people who'd rather shoot marbles!

They say Las Vegas is one of the toughest towns in America. And if you don't believe it, where else have you ever seen a church with a bouncer?

There's only one problem with Las Vegas. It does get hot. One day it got so hot, even the winners were sweating!

LAWNS

I just got my water bill for July. That's all I need—a lawn with a drinking problem.

Maintaining a lawn is battling against impossible odds. Mother Nature is growing crab grass twenty-four hours a day and you're pulling it out two hours a week!

We have one big problem with our lawn—dew on the grass. Dew on the grass! Every morning twenty-two of our neighbors' dogs dew on the grass!

I warned the neighbors, if this keeps up I'm going to do one of two things: either call the dog catcher or put in a pay fence!

LIFE STYLES

The newest trend in American architecture is walled communities for people who want to feel secure—and they really work. I have an uncle who's been living in one of these walled communities for six years now and they've never had one break-in. Maybe you heard of it—Leavenworth.

Well, the people inside don't really call it Leavenworth. They give it a much fancier name—the Walled-Off Astoria.

My wife is one of those modern mothers. She has three rings and six of those clanking bracelets on each arm and she never raises a hand to the children. Raise a hand? She can't even lift it!

I overheard my son trying to figure out if he could afford his own apartment. He was saying to himself, "I'll need $200 for a water bed, $300 for a stereo, $75 for a wine rack, $400 for an air conditioner, $500 for color TV." Then a long pause, followed by, "And maybe I better figure a few extra dollars—for luxuries."

I'm so unlucky, I once got a hernia during a consciousness-raising session.

Yesterday I went to a formal dinner. I knew it was formal. The mustard paddles were sterling.

LUCK

I had one of those weekends where everything went wrong. Like I found out my four-leaf clover isn't a four-leaf clover. It's a two-leaf clover with the mumps!

Do you ever get the feeling that fate was taking a fancy to you—and dropped it?

I've never been lucky—never! I would have been on standby for Noah's Ark.

I've always had bad luck. I once invested $10,000 in a prize dog for breeding purposes. Got him home and he barked with a lisp.

I've never been lucky with girls. Last night I met this gorgeous girl at a party and I said to her, "You're the most dazzling, vivacious, delectable girl I've ever seen. Could I have your phone number?" She said, "Certainly. It's in the book." I said, "Fantastic! And what's your name?" She said, "That's in the book too."

I'm so unlucky, if I traveled 500 miles to see an eclipse of the sun—it would happen at night.

I'm so unlucky, one time I got a paper cut from a get-well card.

I'm so unlucky, one time I threw myself on the mercy of the court—and missed!

I'm so unlucky, if I bought a carnation farm, they'd cancel Mother's Day.

I'm so unlucky, I was walking down Eighth Avenue and a girl asked me, "Do you want to have some fun?" I said, "Yes." So she sold me a joke book.

I'm so unlucky, yesterday I went up to Echo Mountain and yelled, "Helloooo!"—and got an answering service!

I'm so unlucky, I had walking pneumonia and bunions.

MARRIAGE

In marriage, you learn how to pay—either attention or dearly.

I'll tell you what my home life is like. We've got a goldfish that gets to open his mouth more than I do.

I'm the superstitious, old-fashioned type. I believe it's bad luck to see the bride before the wedding—and sometimes for twenty-five years after.

I don't want to start any trouble, but do you realize what the electric blanket is doing to American marriage? It's just another example of science taking away a man's job!

I read that when you marry a Japanese girl she comes with a hope chest. By the time you unwrap all those kimonos, that's what you hope she has.

I've always enjoyed this place because it's a real family hotel. They only admit married couples. You can tell that by the register: "Mr. Smith and Mrs. Jones."

June is the month of weddings. Do you know that, if all the honeymoon couples in America were put end to end, they'd be doing it all wrong?

Misery is your wife complaining about a shortage—and it's your honeymoon.

My wife is always dropping little compliments to me. During our honeymoon she said the way I make love reminds her of a very famous food product. I said, "Wheaties, The Breakfast of Champions?" She said, "No. Minute Rice."

Now there's a new group called Marriage Anonymous. If you feel like proposing, you call up this number and an orthodontist quotes you his rates.

If marriages are made in heaven, I'd like to talk to them about the workmanship on my last one.

You think you have troubles. Two months ago my wife left me for good—and my mother-in-law didn't.

We had a very happy marriage until she found out the Book-of-the-Month Club doesn't hold meetings.

Pacifists are people who are opposed to violence. That's why they never serve in the army, navy, marines, or get married.

My son got married last week and I have to admit that one thing in the wedding ceremony upset me. When he turned to his bride and said, "With all my worldly goods I thee endow" —I couldn't help but think, that could mean my checkbook!

It's just amazing how fast some marriages break up. I saw a bride getting married with curlers in her hair. She wanted to look good for the divorce!

You can tell people are getting married more often by little things—like wash-and-wear wedding gowns.

Teenagers have a problem when they get married. They understand love and honor—but obey is a new word to them.

And during the first month after the wedding, teenagers learn a great and profound truth. That marriage is when—the person who picks up after you—is you!

MASSAGE PARLORS

And now, a special message for all you businessmen in the audience: never bring home work on the weekends! Unless you happen to own a massage parlor.

Everyone has some problem. Take the Venus de Milo. Perfect lips, perfect eyes, perfect shoulders, perfect hips. The world's most beautiful woman! Couldn't get a job in a massage parlor!

You know what I like about England? It has class. Do you know that London has a psychological massage parlor? You go in and the girls undress you mentally!

If you have a good story, stick to it. Like, I know a fella who goes to massage parlors to see the comics.

My uncle has a wonderful time at massage parlors. He's hard of hearing and every time he goes to one they ask him, "Do you want a massage or what?" And he says, "What?"

MEAT

My wife went to the butcher shop. She said she'd be back in either twenty minutes or $20, whichever came first.

I paid $8.00 for lamb chops that were so thin, they came with support panties!

Food prices are so high, even the food knows it. Yesterday I walked past a butcher shop and a tongue stuck itself out at me!

I went into a delicatessen and tongue is selling for $5.00 a pound. Five dollars a pound for tongue! I called up my wife and said, "Let's sell Mother!"

Don't complain. Things could be worse. The Pilgrims could have been thankful over a filet mignon.

Everybody's trying to save. Yesterday we made a meat loaf and stuffed it with the cheapest thing we could find—money!

Personally, I can't get too worked up about all this because, when I was a kid, we also had a meat substitute—hunger.

Last night my wife put a plate of food in front of me for dinner. I said, "What's this?" She said, "A Hamburger Surprise." I said, "What's the surprise?" She said, "Try to find the hamburger."

Is it true the Marquis de Sade is alive and well and marking the prices on hamburger?

People just don't eat meat any more. You think I'm kidding? Steak knives are now being sold with instructions!

I've got a frog in my throat. I'm not complaining. It's the first meat I've had in weeks!

It's ridiculous. The last time I had a good slice of meat was when I cut myself whittling.

And supermarkets are coming up with some strange-looking cuts of meat. I'm not sure whether I'm putting the horse before the cart—or in it!

The butcher has gotten very tricky. For instance, I didn't know he carried horse meat until he sold me a drumstick that was six feet long.

If you think the meat situation is bad now—you ain't seen mutton yet!

MEDICINE

Amnesia is Nature's way of saying, "Forget it!"

As far as I'm concerned, any psychiatrist who charges $100 an hour is a follower of Sigmund Fraud.

The latest trend in psychology is for people to be assertive. Say precisely what you think when you think it and it will completely change the shape of your personality. I agree. I was in a bar once and I said to this truck driver precisely what I thought when I thought it—and it did change the shape of my personality, starting with my nose.

My uncle is an oral surgeon. If you're sick he tells you the name of a good doctor.

I went to a podiatrist who charged me $50. I said, "Doc—$50? It's McDonald's who has golden arches, not me!"

The biggest medical problem in the United States today is supermarket whiplash. You get it from watching the prices go up.

If you really want to speed up the medical process, when you stick out your tongue have your Blue Cross card on it.

We all have a cross to bear in this life, and the way the rates are going up, I think it's Blue!

The only thing I want when I have the flu is tea. A half a cup. I don't have the strength to lift a full one.

I went to England on my vacation and I was so disappointed in socialized medicine. I always thought socialized medicine is when you take off all your clothes—and so does the nurse.

The best thing you can do with most drugs is follow the instructions on the bottle. The one that says: KEEP TIGHTLY CLOSED.

MEDITATION

If you sit still with eyes half closed,
It's known as vegetating;
But if the boss is doing it—
It's then called cogitating.
But now I've found the answer
After hours of ruminating:
You still can sit with eyes half closed—
Just call it meditating!

Meditation is the thing,
Its star is really soaring.
Close your eyes and think deep thoughts;
No fair if you start snoring!

You think you have troubles? The guru who gave me my mantra stutters.

I know this is hard to believe, but my kids are starting a brand-new philosophical movement. It's called Transcendental Aggravation.

MEETINGS

I just figured out why the average prayer takes thirty seconds and the average sales conference takes two hours. God listens.

We try to run a rather informal type of meeting. For instance, we use Bob's Rules of Order.

As any parliamentarian will tell you, a yawn is a motion to adjourn.

I'm afraid we're going to have to bring this cocktail hour to an end and begin our meeting—so would you all please take your seats, remembering that old adage: He who hesitates—is SAUCED!

We'd like to get this meeting started. Would everybody please take their seats? Would everybody please take their seats? Would everybody please take their seats—and put them on chairs!

AFTER OPENING PRAYER: I always feel good about any meeting that begins with a prayer although, the way meat prices are, it can be a problem. I was at a dinner last night that began with a prayer. I bowed my head, closed my eyes and somebody stole my roast beef!

The Program Committee had a little difference of opinion as to how we should begin this meeting. Some of us wanted a short prayer followed by the Treasurer's Report. Others wanted the Treasurer's Report followed by a long prayer.

This is our kickoff meeting of the season. It's called our kickoff meeting because, if some of you don't bring your dues up to date, that's what our Treasurer is going to do.

And now, in keeping with the variety format of our program, I'd like to introduce one of the foremost jugglers of our time— our Treasurer.

We were going to make this a shirt-sleeve session but we decided against it. After last season, who has shirts?

WHEN SOMEONE OFFERS AN OBJECTION TO A POPULAR PLAN: Now you know why this club will never have to worry about burning down. In case of fire, we just call _____ and he'll throw a wet blanket on it.

Did you hear about the women's club president who interrupted their meeting by saying, "There's an exhibitionist standing right outside our door. Sylvia, take off your glasses and speak to him!"

A meeting is like panty hose. It's what you put into it that counts.

Last month we had a membership drive and brought in two new members. That isn't so much a drive as a putt.

MIDDLE AGE

I just got my first set of bifocals and it's a fascinating experience. I step off every curb like I'm testing the water in a pool.

Show me a man who walks with his head held high—and I'll show you a man who hasn't quite gotten used to his bifocals.

Some people are like the bottom half of bifocals. They're always blowing things up out of all proportion.

I used to be a go-getter. I still am, but now I have to make two trips!

Middle age is when your figure is like the stock market. It's all there but lower.

Middle age is when you don't have to own antiques to sit down on something that's fifty years old.

Middle age is when you have the same problem as D'Artagnan—your swash keeps buckling.

Middle age is when you slowly turn from stud to dud.

Youth is when zing go the strings of your heart. Middle age is when jiggle goes the jelly of your belly.

When you're young, all you want is a loaf of bread, a jug of wine and thou. When you're middle-aged, you still want the loaf of bread and the jug of wine—but the thou better be Alka-Seltzer.

They say life begins at forty. I got news. So does arthritis!

When it comes to girls, my nephew is at that awkward age—fifty-two.

Middle age creates terrible problems. For instance, my wife has started wearing elastic stockings and it's very upsetting. All her life she's worried about getting runs. Now she worries about getting blowouts!

When you're my age, you go out to the beach and turn a wonderful color. Blue. It's from holding in your stomach.

Arthritis is when you have get-up-and-oh!

Arthritis is a terrible thing. Every morning I get up at the crick of dawn!

Be honest now. Wasn't life better when *you* had ten speeds and bikes didn't?

MISTAKES

They say we can learn from the mistakes of others. My problem is, I'm always the others.

WHEN YOU COMMIT A FAUX PAS: I couldn't be in any more hot water if my name was Lipton.

A mistake is a lesson on its way to being learned.

When it comes to facing the music, you're looking at a regular Leonard Bernstein!

Do you ever get the feeling you've been voted the Man of the Rear?

Here's the way I feel about my critics: I'd be perfectly willing to turn the other cheek, providing it's my choice of cheek.

MODERN LIVING

I can remember how we all used to look forward to seeing Grandma at Thanksgiving. We still do. She's a go-go dancer in Sun City.

We have one couch that's completely covered with plastic. It's eerie. Last New Year's Eve I spilled a drink on it and it's still there!

And who can take a nap on a couch that's covered with plastic? It's like making it with a shower curtain!

Thanks to plastic, my wife has redecorated three times and she's the only one who knows it!

My wife has a wonderful way of coping with exhibitionists. She just smiles kindly at them and says, "I don't blame you for being upset. Maybe Ralph Nader can get you a better one."

It's so easy to get depressed these days. I know a fella who's been an exhibitionist for twenty-five years—and what does he have to show for it?

We had a terrible thing happen today. The people in the apartment over ours had a leak in their water bed. Well, I think they had a leak in their water bed. Either that or they're trying to paper-train an elephant!

MONEY

A safe is a chastity belt for people who love money.

Remember when people had get-up-and-go and savings didn't?

The trouble with Americans today is they're money mad. Every time they look at what's happening to their money, do they get mad!

Money is the root of all evil. I believe it's the root. Look how it's going into the ground.

People really love money these days. You can tell. I just saw a check that says: DO NOT FOLD, BEND OR FONDLE.

I just saw a dumb sign. It said: COIN LAUNDRY. I don't have mine long enough to get dirty.

It all started in Atlantic City. In the early 1900s, Atlantic City came up with the idea of having people sit in chairs with wheels on them while someone propelled them along the boardwalk. And Americans have been pushed for money ever since!

Absence makes the heart grow fonder—which could explain why I love money.

They say two-dollar bills bring bad luck. Not if you have enough of them.

Personally, I'm always a little suspicious of anyone whose job involves money. My idea of a great treasurer is the Venus de Milo.

For those of you who haven't met our treasurer, he's the one with the gray flannel handcuffs.

Charisma is that indefinable something that a fat, bald, ugly, dull person with $40,000,000 has.

Rich? Name me one other fella whose wallet has stretch marks!

MONEY FLUCTUATIONS

They've always said that "money talks,"
A fact you can determine;
But nowadays what money talks
Is Japanese and German.

Our minister is worried sick about the value of the dollar. He's beginning to see them in collection plates.

Do you realize what all these deficits are doing to the dollar? I keep having this terrible dream in which I want to write down a telephone number, so I ask somebody for a piece of scrap paper—and they hand me a single.

My wife collects miniatures. This morning I gave her a dollar.

I'm really worried. If the dollar loses any more in value, it won't come in stacks—it'll come in rolls.

You can tell the dollar is losing its value in little ways. For instance, I now get my pay check by junk mail.

They say that millions of germs can live on a dollar bill. They're lucky. With me it doesn't even buy coffee!

I wish people wouldn't tell me that I look just the way I did twenty years ago. So does the dollar.

MORALITY

It's amazing how many people who have a solid set of values never use them. I guess they don't want to break up the set.

I'm kinda discouraged. Every time I stand up for what's right —somebody steals my chair.

If you want to know what it's like to be really ignored in this world—put up a STOP sign in Lovers' Lane.

The only difference between the Old and the New Morality is in what girls cross—their legs or their fingers.

Talk about permissiveness, there's a new religion based on the Ten Commandments. Only now they're a multiple choice.

A typical American is someone who gets incensed at politicians charged with bribery and extortion—and then gives his kid fifty cents to turn off the TV and go to bed.

Parents are people who, on occasion, rise to incredible heights of ingenuity. Yesterday I heard a five-year-old kid ask his father, "Dad, what's a hooker?" Dad never even hesitated. He said, "Son, a hooker is a one-fingered pickpocket who steals key rings!"

"Call girl" is such a hard description. Why don't we just say she lives in the finest hotels in town—an hour at a time?

MOTHER'S DAY

Kids! On Mother's Day, why not give Mom a gift she will always remember, always treasure, always be grateful for? Leave!

I can remember when I was a kid. Every year we'd give Mom a great big five-pound box of our favorite candy. . . . Mom always got the first piece—and if she was real quick, the last!

Mother's Day is very confusing to kids. I was twelve years old before I learned that carnations grow in fields—not on one-pound boxes of candy.

Mother's Day is when millions of mothers look at their kids with clenched hands—but at least they're around flowers.

And have you tried to buy a bouquet for Mother's Day? This is the season when the flowers are cut and the customers are clipped.

If you ask me, mothers are the great actresses of our time. Who else can show such delight at getting a 64-ounce bottle of perfume—with a 25¢ label still on it?

Mother's Day is when druggists sell kids the perfume that drives mothers out of their minds and the rest of us out of the room.

The aroma of Mother's Day perfumes is very distinct. I took the stopper out of one, sniffed, and that's what I said to myself, "Distinct!"

Mother's Day perfume is sort of an all-purpose gift. It pleases mothers one day a year—and kills mosquitoes the rest.

Mother's Day perfume has so much alcohol, you don't know whether to decorate it with a ribbon or an olive.

The kids next door told their mother she wasn't to lift a finger on Mother's Day. They were going to do all the cooking. So they got out three pots, two fry pans, a double boiler, three mixing bowls, a chopping board, six measuring spoons, eight serving dishes—and Mom was delighted. She said it was the best Jell-O she ever tasted.

Mother's Day is when the kids say she's the greatest cook in the world—and then make her a dinner that proves it!

The greatest Mother's Day tribute I ever heard came from a very successful business executive. He said, "Yes, I am a self-made man—but the blueprints came from my mother."

MOVIES

Last night I thought I was going to die and my whole life flashed before me. It was awful. I hate B movies.

Let's face it, I lived a very sheltered life. Do you know that I wasn't even allowed to go to the movies—because they showed shorts?

I've been watching Fred Astaire movies for forty years now and there's only one thing that bothers me. He's so meticulous, so precise, so perfect—just once I would have liked to see him stop in the middle of a routine to tie his shoelace!

It's just amazing how Westerns have changed. I saw one where the meanest, toughest, orneriest gunslinger in town was the hairdresser. You may have seen it. It's called *Fastest Spitcurl in the West!*

This Western is so modern, when the settlers get attacked by the Indians, they send out for two things—help and a pizza!

Nobody knows all the troubles the good guys had. I once talked to one of these old Western stars and he said, "It

wasn't easy to wear a white hat on the streets of Dodge City."
I said, "Bandits?" He said, "Pigeons. . . . Why do you think
they called it Dodge City?"

My five-year-old doesn't know it, but every night he refers to
the new movies when he recites the Lord's Prayer. He says,
"Forgive us our trespasses, as we forgive those who press
trash upon us!"

Nowadays movies are where you pay four dollars so that during the intermission you can spend seventy-five cents for a
ten-cent candy bar worth a nickel!

I can always tell when there's a sexy scene in a movie. My
wife leans over and breathes on my glasses.

I have an idea that could shorten the Academy Awards presentations to forty-five minutes. When the winners come up
and say thank you—have them come up and say thank you!

MUGGING

Winter is here. You can tell. Muggers have much colder
hands.

You can tell how many people have colds. Yesterday I was
mugged for my Kleenex.

I won't say how long they expect this crime problem to last,
but they just included muggers under Social Security!

I'm going to sue the phone company. Don't laugh. This is serious. They told me to let my fingers do the walking. Did you
ever have a pinky mugged?

You can't believe what's happening in this town. Yesterday I
was mugged for my police whistle!

When it comes to money, you have to hand it to my uncle. He's a mugger.

MUSIC

Modern music is when you feel like clapping your hands—over your ears.

I just figured out why so many great guitar players come from farms. It's the same stroke you use for plucking chickens!

Do you know why the guitar will never replace the piano as the world's standard instrument? How do you rest a glass of beer on a guitar?

One rock star isn't doing too well. You can tell. You know how most singers use an electric guitar? He has a wind-up.

Do you ever get the feeling that all you need to be a folk singer is an open mind and a closed nose?

They really don't appreciate culture in this town. I knew it the minute I tried to tap dance to Beethoven's Fifth.

Whatever happened to those great old songs, like "We Were Sailing Along on Turhan Bey"?

When I was a kid, I was in a drum and bugle corps that was so bad, the drums carried the tune.

I just figured out why they call them marching bands. If you played like they do, you'd keep moving too!

I used to play the cymbals in a marching band but I had to give it up. Who wants to go through life with a belly button that winces?

One fella had this big instrument around his neck and I asked him, "Is that a tuba?" He said, "No. It's a stethoscope for Orson Welles!"

Believe me, it isn't easy being a tuba player. After every note you have to say: "Excuse me!"

Legend has it that the musicians on the *Titanic* kept playing right up to the very end—and that's true. The drummer was playing with a secretary from the Bronx, the trombonist was playing with a schoolteacher from Des Moines, the—

NEATNESS

I won't say he's a sloppy eater but, to him, finger food is mashed potatoes.

WHEN YOU SPILL SOMETHING ON YOURSELF: You've heard of tie-dyed? I think mine just did.

They say that kids today walk taller than we used to. Of course they walk taller. Everything they own is on the floor!

But, as parents, you have to adjust. For instance, my wife and I used to get upset when we saw our son's brand-new $75 sweater on the rug. But we learned to accept, to compromise, to understand. Now we know that his brand-new $75 sweater isn't *on* the rug. It *is* the rug!

We had a very upsetting day Tuesday. A guest accidentally went into my son's room and we spent the rest of the day seeing if our homeowner's policy covers shock.

I'll say one thing for my son. He has no hang-ups. Everything he owns is on the floor.

The house is six years old. He has a closet and 22 hangers that are brand new.

You want to know how much stuff he has on the floor? We have a ranch house. His room is a duplex!

And kids themselves are so messy. I have a fourteen-year-old. You should see the way this kid dresses. He looks like an explosion in a Salvation Army warehouse!

He says he wants to follow his own life style. Life, maybe. Style, never!

NEIGHBORHOODS

I come from a very poor neighborhood. You know how some people have homing pigeons? We had homing cockroaches.

I'll tell you what this neighborhood is like. The Welcome Wagon is a tank.

We have sort of a Christmas tradition in our neighborhood. Fifty people go from door to door singing Christmas carols. Fifty people! Five for harmony and the rest for protection!

I live in a very friendly neighborhood. People are always willing to take your hand; to take your side; to take your purse!

You've heard of mad money? In my neighborhood, if you carry any, you are!

"Superman is faster than a speeding bullet." Would he be at home in my neighborhood!

I live in a very quiet neighborhood. Very quiet. Where else can you hear people whispering for help?

The couple next door have an interesting family. One boy, two girls and three its.

NERVOUSNESS

Nervous breakdowns show you care.

I was a very timid kid. When I first learned how to crawl, I had knees with training wheels.

I'm so nervous (POINT AT YOUR THROAT). This may look like a bow tie to you. It isn't. One of the butterflies in my stomach got out!

As you can see, I'm a little nervous. I have the same empty, apprehensive feeling in the pit of my stomach as the day I was first introduced to my college roommate—and he lisped.

NEWLYWEDS

Newlyweds who make both ends meet have accomplished two things—a balanced budget and the world's most inexpensive method of birth control.

I have a very important job this winter. I tell newlyweds when their furnace has gone out.

Last year we had a wild New Year's Eve. We made it a Come as You Are party and invited honeymooners.

NEWSPAPERS

I'm at that age where the only section of the paper I approve of is called "25 YEARS AGO TODAY."

I'm not saying this man is a bad reporter. All I'm saying is, if he had been Moses, what we'd have today is the Six Commandments.

I once wanted to write a letter to the *Times* on the great need for resourcefulness in our society—but I couldn't find their address.

The trouble with giving someone the title of Associate Editor is—you have to be very careful when you abbreviate it.

NEW YEAR

I'm not surprised the twentieth century is beginning to look a little tired. It's eighty-three.

I wish you just one thing for the New Year: may your troubles last as long as your resolutions!

First, I want to wish you a happy and prosperous and wonderful New Year. I want to do it right now—before we know better.

I've listened to dozens of economists and planners and government officials, and so far my dog is the only one who has made an accurate prediction for the New Year. He says, "Rough!"

It's just frightening the way things are going. I happen to know the 19——— calendars only go up to March.

They always show those pictures of 19——— going out as a real old man and I want to tell you something: 19——— was enough to age anybody!

On New Year's Day, we always open all those gift packages of food people sent at Christmas. You know the ones—where they put in four ounces of cheese; three ounces of jelly; and ten pounds of profit?

I opened one package—this big. (INDICATE LARGE.) I won't say how much food was inside but I had to burp from memory!

But one year someone sent us a case of brandied fruit and that was great. First time I've ever been under the influence of plums!

New Year's Day is great for the ecology. Every year I recycle my resolutions.

One of my resolutions is to improve my mind. In fact, I just joined a combination consciousness-raising and bowling club.

NEW YEAR'S EVE

Do you realize that every New Year's Eve 40,000,000 Americans go out to New Year's Eve parties? Ladies and gentlemen, these are staggering figures!

Procrastination is when you see the second hand approaching the hour of midnight on New Year's Eve—and wonder who to invite to the party.

Last New Year's Eve a drunk got on the (LOCAL) bus, staggered up the aisle, flopped into a seat beside this little old lady. She looked him up and down, sniffed and said, "I've got news for you. You're going straight to hell!" The drunk jumped up and said, "Good heavens, I'm on the wrong bus!"

New Year's Eve is when you can tell the truly dedicated people in Washington. They're the ones who get up and dance to the Congressional Record.

On New Year's Eve happiness is a night club where your check is as small as your table.

On New Year's Eve you can always tell the people with strength of mind. They're the ones who go to a topless night club and watch the clock!

Vanity once wrecked the greatest New Year's Eve party I ever went to. I wanted to look suave and debonair, so I didn't wear my glasses. Then, at the stroke of midnight, I poured champagne into a girl's slipper—and her foot was still in it. . . . I want to tell you something. Nineteen sixty-nine was a great year for wine. For toes, not so good!

December 31st is when you play a kissing game with six gorgeous girls. It's called New Year's Eve roulette. Five are breathing heavy with passion—and one with flu.

Now at the stroke of midnight I want you to give a long, smoldering, passionate kiss to the one you love most. And if your wife is handy, give her a peck too!

I don't want to seem overly sentimental, but at the stroke of midnight on New Year's Eve I went over and kissed the warmest, most precious part of my life—our fuel tank.

I started to get suspicious of my wife when she wore curlers to a New Year's Eve party. She wanted to look good for the milkman!

We're so broke, my wife and I stayed home and toasted the New Year. She had rye and I had whole wheat.

Did I ever tell you about the time I was arrested on New Year's Eve for trying to lift a cup of cheer? It was a C cup.

I always go to New Year's Eve parties Jolly Giant style. I start off "Ho, ho, ho!" and I end up green!

Every New Year's Eve I feel like the needles on a Christmas tree. I start off bright and shiny and neat—and the next thing I know, I'm on the floor.

NEW YORK CITY

New York City is where we paid $24 for Manhattan Island and thought we had cheated the Indians.

I don't know why they say New York is so expensive. For only $18 a day I have accommodations facing Central Park. The reason it's facing Central Park—it's a bench.

I just read a book that tells you how you can come to New York City and live on $5.00 a day. When you get off the bus, you mug a cop!

They say New York is overcrowded, which is ridiculous. Just last night I had a mugger all to myself.

New York City has something for everyone. Greenwich Village is the land of the free and Wall Street is the home of the brave.

They really have the Christmas spirit in New York. I was in the subway and a sign said: MERRY NO SMOKING AND SPITTING.

NONSENSE

Would anybody like to sign a petition for pun control?

What makes everybody so sure this is an eclipse? The way things are going, maybe the sun just can't stand the sight of us.

I don't fly because I'm afraid of height. Really afraid of height. I get dizzy looking over the edge of a belly button.

They say an army travels on its stomach. I didn't believe that until I saw a radial belly button!

A belly button is a very useful part of your anatomy. Ask anyone who is smoking in bed and can't find an ash tray.

They just built a roller coaster for people who live in San Francisco. It's level.

It doesn't make sense. Like getting a mouth transplant from Howard Cosell.

And now I would like to quote from one of the greatest writers of all time, Anonymous!

I'm now forty-eight years old and one thing has always bothered me. How do you tell if a yodeler has hiccups?

NOSTALGIA

Sometimes I get nostalgic for the fifties. I'm so broke, I even get nostalgic for the twenties, tens and fives.

Enjoy yourself. If you don't, what'll you be nostalgic about in 1990?

Whatever happened to the good old days, when the only rip-offs were paper towels?

We tend to forget one of the reasons why they were called "the good old days." The days were old but we weren't.

Whatever happened to all those wonderful candies kids used to eat? Remember that candy that used to come in a little tin cup plus the little tin spoon with the sharp edges? I think it came in three flavors—vanilla, chocolate and blood!

And how about those pink marshmallow bananas? Remember them? You ate a half dozen and you lost three things—your color, your appetite and your lunch!

Then there were candy buttons. Those long strips of paper

with candy glued to them. Every day I used to eat one pound of candy and three pounds of paper! . . . I ate so much paper, I didn't burp, I rattled!

But everybody's favorite was bubble gum. I blew bubbles four hours a day right up to the time I was sixteen. Then I found out a pucker had better uses!

NUDE BEACHES

A newspaper editor got a fascinating phone call the other day. The voice on the other end said, "How dare you put down nude bathing beaches? Nude bathing beaches are the greatest thing to come along in years! What this country needs is more nude bathing beaches!" The editor said, "I'm sorry but I can hardly hear you. Would you speak a little louder?" The voice said, "I can't. I'm a mosquito!"

I saw one bather at a nude beach—seventy years old! And she was proud of it. She said, "What do you think of my birthday suit?" I said, "It needs ironing."

Nude bathing beaches are all the rage;
They're really creating a stir.
My wife went once but never again—
Somebody called her "Sir"!

You know what's so great about going to a nude beach? Your outfit is never out of style!

Going to a nude bathing beach is a unique experience. It's the only way I know to have red cheeks in August.

Thanks to nude bathing beaches, for the first time in history people with big belly buttons are in demand. Where else are you going to keep the car keys?

One beach has girl life guards and even they're nude. It was great until they passed that new rule: you can't drown without your wife's permission!

NUDISTS

Wash and wear is nothing new. Look at nudists.

My wife always wanted to be a nudist but one thing stopped her. Her birthday suit seems to have so much more material than anybody else's.

You can count on three terrible shocks when becoming a nudist. One is the first time you take off all your clothes. The other two are sitting down on a cold marble bench.

Roses are red,
Violets are blue.
Violet is a nudist in Alaska.

I love to watch those feats that make you gasp a "Golly gee!" Like sliding down the banister in a nudist colony!

Tonight we will debate one of the great and burning issues of our time: why do they have closets in nudist camps?

Modesty is a guitar player in a nudist camp.

I know a camp that's so exclusive, you have to wear a tie to get in. What makes it so crazy—it's a nudist camp!

If you've never been to a nudist camp, it's sort of a McDonald's for mosquitoes.

I think any girl who gets painted in the nude deserves a lot of credit. Those brushes tickle!

After every election you overhear such wild conversations.

Like: "My neighbor couldn't wait to take off his _____ button."

"He's a sore loser?"

"No. He's a nudist."

NURSES

Hospitals are so impersonal. You can't believe the things nurses do to you while discussing the weather. . . . I mean, it's one thing to be familiar, but I didn't know if I was having my first operation or second honeymoon!

And after all this they suddenly get coy. When they give you a bed bath, they wash 95% of you with a damp cloth and then, when they get to the most interesting part, they let you finish the job. That's like being invited down to the wine cellar for ginger ale!

A practical nurse once told me, "If you really want to get attention in a hospital, give a little thought to T.L.C." I said, "Tender Loving Care?" She said, "No. T.L.C. Try Leaving Cash!"

OFFICE

I work in a very mellow office. For instance, we have a little red box on the wall. It says: IN CASE OF FIRE, BREAK GLASS. You know what's inside? Marshmallows!

But we do have a fantastic fire alarm system. The minute somebody gets fired, the whole office knows about it.

The big thing today is productivity. For instance, we have

something in our office that has increased productivity 75%. It's a coin-operated water cooler.

OIL

I don't want to brag, but yesterday I lit my cigar with a hundred-dollar bill. It was from my oil dealer.

I paid our heating oil bill today. Tell me, how can you make ends meet when one of them is in Saudi Arabia?

Two ostriches are standing with their heads in the sand: One ostrich says, "Tell me, why are we always doing this?" And the other ostrich says, "I don't know about you, but I'm looking for oil!"

There are a lot of problems besetting the oil industry, but as the head of a company with earnings of $2,000,000,000 recently said, "It's a living."

Life is like an oil well. Some of us get the oil. Some of us get the shaft.

They're now charging $_____ a barrel for oil, which is ridiculous. Personally, I can't see paying $_____ for a barrel of anything you can't serve with pretzels.

OLD AGE

I always thought the Golden Oldies was a nude beach at Sun City.

I was born old. I was the only kid who ever had liver spots on his acne.

Old age is when you can't quite decide whether you've saved too little or stayed too long.

I've been buying stocks for twenty years to provide for my old age. I now call it my crash program.

Stocks no longer provide for your old age but they do hasten its arrival.

It isn't easy to be a senior citizen. You ever run out of Poli-Grip during a bagel-eating contest?

You know you're getting old when even your hot flashes are lukewarm.

Seventy is when your vital juices are prune.

My transistor radio and my arteries have one thing in common. They're both solid state.

I've reached that age when I have to put on my glasses just to think.

I don't park with girls any more. At my age it's too embarrassing—particularly when you run out of gas—after you run out of gas.

I'll never forget the first time I realized I was growing older. It was when I spent five minutes looking at a picture of a horse before I realized who was on it—Lady Godiva!

Have you noticed that just about the time you're over the hill your brakes give out?

On average, a wife lives seven years longer than her husband. Six of them are spent looking for the will.

When your hair has turned to silver,
And your teeth have turned to gold;
Make sure you're growing wiser—
Instead of merely old!

I won't say how old I am, but last week I was in an antique shop and three people tried to buy me!

My neighbor has arrived at the age where, if he drops $10 in the collection plate, it's not a contribution—it's an investment.

IF YOU'RE BALD: I bought that electric comb with the little light on it. With my hair, the problem isn't combing it. It's finding it.

ORGIES

My favorite recollection of the summer was this conversation overheard at a resort:
"Would you care to join us? We need a fourth."
"Bridge?"
"No. Orgy!"

An orgy is no-fault sex.

I just got an invitation to an orgy. I think they want an answer. In the corner it says R.S.B.V.D.

My wife says we ought to share our interests, so starting next Saturday night we are. We're holding a combination orgy and Tupperware party.

People are always putting me down. Why, just yesterday I was put out of a place for not wearing a tie. What made it even worse, it was an orgy.

OSTENTATION

Don't you just hate people who try to make you feel inferior? I was telling my wife about our neighbor. He's painting his house and giving it two coats. She said, "Lots of people give their house two coats." I said, "Mink?"

It's all right to have a big house, but who has a walk-in mailbox?

Rich? Who else do you know has a Gucci Christmas tree?

Did you hear about the rich Texan who never has to wear glasses when watching television? He has a prescription picture tube!

Everybody is so money-conscious these days. I have a friend who calls his home "El Rancho 245 Grande."

Rich? He has the Vitamin E concession for Niagara Falls!

Ostentation is a motor home with an elevator.

Don't you just hate people who put on airs? My neighbor says he's been going South for the winter—and he has. The unemployment office is downtown.

OVERWEIGHT

I didn't realize how much influence the United States had on the rest of the world until I read about low-cal whale blubber for fat Eskimos.

Logic is when you come to the conclusion that either you're gaining weight or the holes in your belt are healing up.

You know you've put on too much weight when you try to loosen your belt and you can't find it.

I bought one of those health belts for the stomach that pulls in and redistributes your fat—and it really works. My waistline is now 34—and so are my ankles.

Misery is when you break two things—your diet and the bathroom scale.

There are certain telltale little signs that you're gaining weight—like when you have to use the full-length mirror sideways.

There's no use arguing. You're overweight if that cute little dimple on your knee is your belly button.

Isn't it embarrassing when you're a few pounds overweight and your stomach hangs a little over your trunks? A little over my trunks? I need a bookmark to find the zipper!

I won't say how much weight I've gained, but I have wide neckties that look narrow.

Lately I've found that every time I want to rest on my laurels I need wider laurels.

My doctor really knows how to make a point. He said, "The first thing I want you to do is stop heavy lifting." I said, "How do I do that?" He said, "Lose forty pounds!"

I joined a health club to lose weight and it really worked. Just like that they took off $245 from around the wallet.

I've counted so many calories, the only thing that's lost weight is my index finger.

WHEN SOMEBODY JOKES ABOUT YOUR WEIGHT: Don't you just hate people who make fun at your expanse?

PARTIES

I've got a wife who loves to throw parties. Especially around this time of the year. Like for the last three weeks, the bedspread in our room has been coats!

Isn't it great the way people just walk in and throw their coats on your bed? Yesterday I was taking a nap and before I knew it I had a mouthful of mink!

And do you know what the most dangerous time in any American household is? Thirty-five minutes before company is supposed to arrive. If you're a husband, suddenly the whole house is off limits!

We had a party last night, and thirty-five minutes before the first doorbell, my wife yelled in: "Where are you?" I said: "I'm standing in the living room." She said: "On the rug?" I said: "No, I'm hanging by my cummerbund from the chandelier!" . . . She said: "Good. Don't make footprints!"

And perish forbid, I should eat any of the potato chips. They're for company! Friends, do you know what it is to stand in an empty living room—potato chips to the right of you, popcorn to the left of you, two pounds of cashew nuts in front of you—and you're hooked on salt? . . . I tell you, my mouth watered so bad—my teeth went down for the third time!

"Don't eat the food. It's for company. Don't drink the liquor. It's for company. Don't use the ash trays. They're for company!" Suddenly you don't have a home any more. It's Leavenworth with guest towels!

Guest towels! Aren't they the most ridiculous things? When—when, I ask you, have you ever seen a used guest towel? . . . Guest towels are like the back-row seats in a burlesque house. You only use them if you have no other choice!

You think I'm kidding? The next time you have a party—put three guest towels and a shower curtain in the bathroom—and see which gets wetter!

PERSONALITIES

Do you ever get the feeling _____ was inoculated against charisma?

TALKATIVE PERSON: This is ridiculous. I didn't know they made pacemakers for tongues!

I wish people wouldn't call me "one in a million." I always wonder if they're grading on a curve.

I'm not what you might call the romantic type. If I put my ear to a sea shell, what it reminds me of is Alka-Seltzer.

My problem is concentration. The only time I can keep my mind on two things at the same time—is during a Dolly Parton concert.

Women have always adored me. I'll tell you how popular I am with women—I have two navels!

You think that's something? I know a fella who has three navels. His mother was crazy for bowling.

All my life I've been a loser. I ask you—who else has a parakeet with bad breath?

I'm so unpopular, when whippoorwills call, it's collect!

I just met the world's most amazing person. He writes the Gettysburg Address on the head of a pin. What makes it so amazing, he uses a crayon!

Good-natured? He smiles for X-ray pictures!

Strong? You know how some men can open train windows? He can open plane windows!

Sloppy? He'd need a bib just to fast!

PHILOSOPHY

Don't give till it hurts. Give till it feels good!

I don't agree with the philosophy that the end justifies the means. Only once did I see an end that justified the means and she said no.

ATHEISTS FALL ON THEIR FAITH!

A smile is a carnation in the buttonhole of life.

People who try to snatch victory from the jaws of defeat never lose hope. Just fingers!

"Tomorrow is the first day of the rest of your life." Which is a problem. Nobody likes to hire beginners.

They said that it could not be done,
But within me I knew I might;
So I tried and tried and tried and tried,
You know something? They were right!

Do you ever get the feeling that you're starting off on the wrong foot—and you're a centipede?

People who want to put you in on the ground floor never tell you there's a basement.

There has to be something wrong with a world where you have to die to get perpetual care.

It is better to be in the missionary position than never to have any religion at all.

As any African elephant hunter will tell you—it's all right to have a big trap, but you have to know when to close it.

I can't understand why people work so hard to get a place in the sun. What has it done for Egypt?

I've always been grateful for the name Bob. I have little else—but all of my aspirins are monogrammed!

If the world changes any faster, pretty soon the good old days will be 2:00 P.M.

Life is a game. My problem is I'm playing it like the (CELLAR TEAM).

Beware the person who tries to take a weight off your mind. It might just be a subtle way of calling you a fathead.

A tradition is what you have when you're too lazy to think up something new.

It's all right to wrestle with your conscience, but don't make it two falls out of three.

It doesn't make sense, like playing strip solitaire.

Life is like opening a new shirt. Whenever you think you've found all the pins, there's one more left to stick you.

This is a lollipop world. Everybody's trying to get their licks in.

Do you ever get the feeling that life is a violin solo and you're wearing mittens?

Life is like spaghetti cooked *al dente*. It's hard.

I always try to count my blessings—but I'm no good at fractions.

The ladder of success may now be an elevator—but it's still self-service.

My neighbor has become calm, confident, and has an entirely new outlook on life. It all happened that day he discovered a brand-new philosophy—Transcendental Adultery.

Arrogance is the humility of the insecure.

When you live in the lap of luxury, there's never a long-term lease.

When you buy trouble, there's never a rebate.

People who say, "Nothing is impossible," have never tried to make a date with a recorded announcement.

I can do without anything in this world except self-indulgence.

Life is a cabaret—and as you grow older, you spend more and more time in the washroom.

Sometimes I get the feeling we laugh by the inch and cry by the foot.

Belly dancers are people who use body language—and stutter.

PLANTS

I understand you can talk to plants. (GO OVER TO ANY PLANT OR FLOWERS NEAR THE MIKE AND SAY): Laugh it up!

They say that plants are almost human and that's right. I have a potted plant that's crazy about Dean Martin.

They say that plants need warmth and love. I know, but I feel slighted. On Valentine's Day my geranium got six more cards than I did.

I started to talk to my plants. For two weeks I said warm, affectionate, loving things to them. Frankly, I've only noticed one difference. Now, when I come into the room, my roses cross their stems.

I try to say sweet, loving things to my plants and most of the time it works. My rubber, cactus and snake plants are doing fine—but my petunias know what a liar I am.

I believe that talking to plants does help. Every day I go up to my roses and say, "Grow, roses, grow!" Then I go up to my petunias and say, "Grow, petunias, grow!" Then I go up to my pansies and say, "Grow, thweety, grow!"

I think we're carrying this talking to plants too far. I mean, I just saw a gladiolus with a hearing aid.

PLAYBOY

You have to be very careful during an eclipse. The sun is like the centerfold of *Playboy* when your wife is in the room. It's dangerous to look directly at it.

They say a cheetah is the fastest mammal. That's not so. The fastest mammal is a husband folding up the center of *Playboy* when his wife walks into the room.

If you're nearsighted, *Playboy* is the ideal magazine to read. The letters are normal but the figures are oversize.

You know what's wrong with those *Playboy* calendars? They're impractical. By the time you get down to looking at the numbers, there's something covering your glasses. Steam!

You know what would be interesting? A braille edition of *Playboy*.

PLUMBERS

On Monday a doctor charged me $15 to fix my poor circulation. On Tuesday a plumber charged me $150 to fix my frozen water pipes. There's a moral to this story: if you let anything harden, better it should be your arteries!

Show me a fella who has water on the knee and I'll show you a homeowner who tried to save $40 an hour on a plumber.

Our plumber is very fair. He only charges $7.00 an hour—but I think it starts from the day he was born.

There's even a new gambling game called Plumbers' Roulette. You call six plumbers and one of them has a kid who needs orthodonture.

It always used to bother me how dirty and messy and grimy plumbers are, but then one of them explained the psychology of it. He said, "The biggest problem a plumber has is kibitzing. So whenever I enter a house, the first thing I do is shake hands with every member of the family. And by the time they finish washing the grease off—I'm through!"

He's a very conscientious plumber. One time I phoned him about frozen pipes and an hour later he called to say he couldn't get through the snow. But the next time he called he said he could get through the snow. Why not? It was August!

POLITICS

I kept my ear to the ground,
Like politicians have always said.
I kept my ear to the ground—
And somebody stepped on my head!

A lot more people would be interested in politics if the Electoral College had a football team.

What this country really needs is more people giving up politics—but still staying in office.

I just picked up a fantastic bargain in a secondhand car. It was only used by (LOSING PRESIDENTIAL CANDIDATE) for inaugural parades.

In politics it's amazing how fast under-the-table can make you over-the-hill.

A lot of politicians who are as American as apple pie still want to get their slice.

They say our dollar buys less than ever before. I didn't believe it until I saw the candidates for mayor.

I just got back from a $100-a-plate dinner. I know a bargain when I see one.

Yesterday I took my wife to a $100-a-plate dinner. I had to. Who can afford restaurants?

Have you ever gone to a $100-a-plate dinner? No matter how worthy the cause is, it's an eerie feeling to drop a french fry and think, "There goes a buck!"

I once went to a political dinner and I made the most unnecessary request in history. I asked a senator to hand me the baloney.

POLLUTION

A little poem dedicated to smog:
            I think that I shall never see—

The smog must be getting worse. Yesterday the Hollywood After Dark tour started at noon!

The only way we're going to make it through this winter is to use fuels that increase pollution. The choice is ours—wheezing or freezing!

The Civil War was the difference between the Blue and the Gray. Thanks to pollution, we still have a difference between the Blue and the Gray. The Blue are people who breathe the air and the Gray are people who wear it.

I'll tell you how bad air pollution is. I can remember when "As I live and breathe" was a statement instead of a choice.

I guess you heard what happened to the Goodyear blimp. They filled it with Los Angeles air and it died.

I'm really getting worried about water pollution. I mean, I don't mind having a ring around the bathtub, but at least it should be *after* you take the bath.

I'll tell you what the water is like in this town. I have a goldfish that takes Tums!

POSTAL RATE INCREASES

I refuse to be intimidated by the new postal rates. I lick stamps. Stamps don't lick me!

If first-class mail goes up again the most popular song in town will be "Let Me *Call* You, Sweetheart—I Can't Afford to Write."

I know how to put off a postal increase for two years. Have them request it by mail.

According to one economist, at the present rate of inflation, it could go to $500 an ounce. Not gold—postage!

They figure that by the year 2000 it could cost as much as 75¢ to mail a letter. Big deal! That's what it costs now. Twenty cents to mail it and 55¢ for phone calls to see if it arrived.

I don't mind paying _____ cents to mail a letter because you get something for it—aggravation!

I don't know about you, but as a result of the postal increase I've written my last Letter to the Editor. I just can't see spending _____ cents to put in my two cents' worth.

The post office is raising its basic rate again—which makes sense. Do you know what it costs these days to lose a letter?

POST OFFICES

DON'T SPEED UP THE POST OFFICE—SLOW DOWN LIFE!

I just learned a terrible thing about letter carriers. Everybody thinks they wear gray uniforms. They're really black uniforms. By the time they deliver those letters, they've *turned* gray!

I don't want to complain about the post office, but when was the last time you got a Get Well card while you were still sick?

I once asked a postal official, "How is it that in London mail is delivered the same day, but in this country it takes as long as a week?" And he came up with a very interesting answer: "Huh?"

I have my own ideas on how to speed up the post office. Send *Playboy* in sealed envelopes.

I keep trying to convince the post office that a baby takes nine months to be delivered—a letter shouldn't.

But thanks to the latest pay increase, postal workers are now ablaze with enthusiasm. You can tell. They're yawning much faster.

I think that I shall never see,
A mailman hurrying to me.

The postal service is having terrible problems with deliveries
and it's spreading. I know a letter carrier whose wife is in her
fourteenth month.

It's a real problem with the post office. If you get an envelope
with a yellow stamp—you don't know if it's ink or age.

Do you think this was a typo? One of our customers said he
was sending us an order by U. S. Snail.

I've had it with mail deliveries. If our dog doesn't bite the
postman, I will!

But have you noticed the post office is much more honest than
it was? I brought in a package and I said to the clerk, "It's
rare imported crystal." He said, "Oh, was it?"

Yesterday I did something I always wanted to do. I congrat-
ulated a parcel post clerk on doing a bang-up job!

Now here's my plan to get rid of the recession: We carefully
wrap it up, seal it with tape, tie it with cord, mark it fragile,
insure it, take it to the post office—and it will never be heard
from again.

The post office has added many modern innovations. For instance, on postage stamps, I have a sneaking suspicion they've
added Teflon to the glue.

I know a postmaster who has never gone to an X-rated movie.
He claims he sees enough things unzipped as it is.

Talk about bargains, what about the post office? Where else
can you mail a letter for 20¢—and have half a million people
work eleven days to deliver it?

POVERTY

My problem is: life is a cabaret—and I don't even have a quarter for the washroom.

Poverty is catching. You can get it from Internal Revenue.

Have you noticed, when your savings go down the drain, you never need Sani-Flush?

If you're living on a pension, the only way you can survive is to eliminate a few things each month—like the last nineteen days.

I don't go out to restaurants any more. It's because of that old saying: Never eat on an empty pocket!

I come from a very poor family. When I was a kid the only sport I ever went out for was Little League Eating.

We were so poor, I was twenty-two before I heard the word "leftovers."

We were so poor, we had to borrow money just to get on relief!

We were so poor, every morning the garbage man drove up and said, "Pick up or delivery?"

We were so poor, burglars used to break in and leave things!

My family may have been poor, but we had one thing in common with the Rockefellers. The Rockefellers had a boat that slept six, and we also had something that slept six—a mattress!

We were so poor, the tooth fairy used to leave I.O.U.s!

My parents had a strange sense of humor. One time I got a quarter for my allowance so I put it under my pillow. The next morning I woke up and what do you think was there? A tooth!

I was telling my wife, "We were so poor, for five years we ate off of paper plates." She said, "Lots of people eat off of paper plates." I said, "The same ones?"

We've arrived at the point where my wife has me eating out of her hands. Who can afford dishes?

PRAYER

I never pray for money. I figure the Lord is my shepherd, not my banker.

You never know what to expect in public speaking. One time I had just started my speech when I heard two officials at the head table start a violent argument in whispers. All I could really hear was one club officer saying to the other, "The prayer! Damn it to hell, you forgot the prayer!"

A silent prayer at a banquet is when everybody bows their heads and listens to the plates in the kitchen.

PRESIDENTS

George Washington wore boots, tight pants, a ruffled shirt and a curly wig. In 1789 he ran for President. In San Francisco he'd run for his life!

It was a very dramatic moment in Washington when the White House chaplain stood up and said, "It is now official. _____ will be our President for another four years. Let us pray!"

At one time or another, every President has to be reminded of the fact that the White House has a landlord—us!

You're all familiar with the invention of the wheel. Well, Inaugural Day is when we celebrate another great achievement —the invention of the big wheel!

Washington, D.C., police are looking for the prankster who took a department store sign saying: JANUARY CLEARANCE— and put it in front of the White House.

Psychiatrists say it's very destructive to threaten your kids. For instance, never tell them they could grow up to be President.

If you don't think real estate has gone up, look what the White House is costing us.

PRICES

I just saw the saddest classified ad. It said: FOR SALE. UNUSED JAR OF STEAK SAUCE. GOING ON SOCIAL SECURITY.

Hawaii is where everything is Aloha but prices.

Nowadays, the first thing to do when buying a suit is find out where the fitting room is. Because, when you learn the price, are you gonna throw one!

I don't mind pulling in my belt a little but I don't want to look like an hourglass either.

For those of you who drink to forget—the price of amnesia has gone up $2.00 a fifth.

PRICES (FOOD)

Something's gotta be done about food prices. Let's not make eating a spectator sport.

You want to know what food prices are like? I just saw a Brink's shopping bag!

They say that, when you eat Chinese food, an hour later you're hungry again. With my pay check, that happens with American food too.

I like the official who said the answer to the problem of high food prices is, we should eat less. I saw him yesterday standing around and burping under an assumed name.

I was surprised to see the manager of the supermarket at the monthly meeting of our Horticultural Club. I thought he only raised prices.

Do you realize that, if the guy who marks up prices in the supermarket was ever murdered, there'd be 200,000,000 suspects?

Our problem is, we saved our money for a rainy day but the supermarket keeps seeding the clouds.

I don't know where we'll go on our vacation. Last year we went to London and watched the Changing of the Guard. This year we may just go to the supermarket and watch the Changing of the Prices.

And those discount coupons are really great. They bring the price of things down to what it would have been if they didn't have to go to the expense of printing all those discount coupons.

Food prices have proven one thing—you don't have to play poker to get a fast shuffle.

Food prices have even affected Easter-egg hunts. Remember when you used to hunt for eggs to get a prize? Now you hunt for eggs to get the eggs!

Food prices are changing our whole way of life. Yesterday I told my kid, "Eat your dessert or you won't get any meat!"

They say the price of bread could go up to $2.00 a loaf. I didn't believe it until I got a roast beef sandwich on pastrami.

Two dollars a loaf. Now I know why they call it cracked wheat. That's what you have to be to pay it.

The whole world is upside down. I can remember when we ate bread because we were poor. Now we're poor because we eat bread.

Believe me, when a loaf of rye costs more than a shot of rye, it's enough to make you drink.

Some people cast bread upon the waters. Not me. I cast $5.00 bills. It's cheaper.

Food is so expensive, our local bank caught a teller who had embezzled $100,000. What gave him away is, one day he burped.

We're living in a time when even average people are having breakfast in bed. When they realize what it's costing them, they get sick!

Food prices are ridiculous. I can remember when a 22-pound turkey came with giblets. Now it comes with a second mortgage.

I woke up in the middle of the night and there was a strange transparent figure standing at the foot of my bed wailing, "Eighty-nine cents a pound!" It was the Ghost of Pork Chop Past!

My wife tries to save money by getting unpopular cuts of meat. For instance, for the last few weeks we've had ankle of lamb.

Two senior citizens, living on Social Security, were standing in front of a butcher's window and one was pointing excitedly at a piece of sirloin. He said, "See! See! That's the stuff I've been telling you about!"

The best way to bring down food prices, lose weight and keep out of trouble—is given in an old Southern expression: "Well, shut my mouth!"

RAILROADS

They're trying to push railroads as an alternative to flying. My friends, I rode on a train last week and it is an alternative to flying—but only if the stagecoach isn't running.

I won't say what this train looked like, but I haven't been so depressed walking down an aisle since I got married.

If this train had been a building, it would have been condemned. . . . Really, it's the first time I've ever been in a 60-mile-an-hour slum!

There's a certain casual look to railroad cars these days. I don't know who maintains the upholstery on the seats but I think it's Jack the Ripper.

And the windows don't seem to get cleaned too often. Like, the only time you know there's daylight outside is after a crash.

Sometimes I think the railroads don't wash the windows on purpose. That way, you can't look out of them, see another train and say, "Omigod, I'm riding on *that*?"

But one of the definite advantages of trains is that they do let you off in the old downtown part of cities—which is just great. If it wasn't for trains, muggers would have to commute.

But the railroads do try to amuse you by passing out a little monthly humor sheet they publish. It's called a timetable.

A railroad timetable is fascinating because it's so precise. It tells you that you'll arrive in Chicago at exactly 10:15 A.M.—give or take a few weeks.

I was on one train that was so late—if my wife was this late, we'd be out pricing bassinets!

And the conductors are so helpful. I said, "What time does this train get to Chicago?" He said, "Eleven oh two." I said, "The timetable says it gets there at ten-fifteen." He said, "So take the timetable!"

I said, "Is there anything I could take to get me to Chicago sooner?" He said, "Sure. The first car."

Now the first thing you notice about trains is there's a certain amount of rocking and swaying and shaking and jerking motion. You can always tell an experienced train rider because he never orders a soup that doesn't match his pants.

I've spilled so much soup into my lap, it's embarrassing. How do you explain to your tailor a rusty zipper?

It's ridiculous. You go into any railroad dining car and it always looks the same—like a convention of bed-wetters!

I once asked a railroad man what caused trains to shake like that and he said, "It's the French painter syndrome." I said, "What French painter could cause a train to shake?" He said, "Tooloose La Track!"

Most trains today don't have dining cars, they have snack bars. Which is also an experience, because you're never quite sure how old the food really is. For instance, I had a liverwurst sandwich that came with a pickle and an N.R.A. sticker.

RAIN

If those deodorants really keep you dry, why are they spraying them on armpits—when it's Seattle that really needs it?

I won't say it rains a lot in Seattle. Let's just put it this way: Seattle is great for anyone who always wanted to live in a carwash.

In Seattle people have learned to live with rain. Where else can you see someone getting married in a rubber tuxedo?

RAINY WEATHER: How about this weather? This is called supermarket rain. You can't go through it without getting soaked.

HEAVY RAIN: Isn't this rain something? I just saw a drunk who was being saved by the Salvation Navy!

RECESSIONS

A government economist said we would not have a recession and I believe it. We're just going to have a boom with a lousy sense of direction.

A recession is what takes the wind out of your sales.

A recession is when your balance sheet suffers from vertigo.

It isn't easy being a salesman during a recession. I know a salesman who died, went to hell and never knew the difference.

You can always tell when we're in a recession. It's when the sales manager asks you how you want your expense account allowance—heads or tails?

You can tell it's a recession. Last night my wife turned to me and said, "Take in the garbage!"

The recession may be coming to a halt but it sure isn't leaving skid marks.

You can tell how quickly the recession started by little things.

For instance, I keep our $1500 season subscription to the opera in the same envelope as my unemployment card.

My neighbor is a pessimist. He says, "The first time I hear an economist who's out of work, just had his car repossessed and is two pay checks behind on his mortgage say that the recession has ended—*then* I'll celebrate!"

My mother used to economize by buying things like day-old bread. Have you ever eaten day-old bread? I was sixteen before I found out that toast is supposed to crunch and bread isn't.

I'll tell you how bad things are. Nowadays if you see someone biting their nails, it's not nerves—it's lunch!

Things are so bad, our local funeral parlor is running a one-cent sale. For an extra penny you can take a friend.

RECYCLING

When it comes to conservation, you just can't beat the stock market. It's just amazing the way it keeps recycling fear.

Summer TV is the perfect example of recycling. It turns me off and I turn it off.

Recycling is a mosquito biting Dracula on the neck.

I don't want to brag, but I happen to be an expert on recycling. I keep falling off.

Recycling would be showing the first X-rated movie on television. You turn it on and it turns you on.

When it comes to recycling, you just can't beat TV soap operas and what they've done with plots.

RELATIONSHIPS

The reason the Garden of Eden was called Paradise is—Adam was a man, Eve was a woman, and the headache hadn't been invented yet.

Revolution is when it's all over quickly. Evolution is when it takes a long time. It's kinda like what happens to your sex life.

It's always upsetting when you behave like a perfect gentleman on your first date—then you take her home and find out she has a monogrammed trapeze.

I must have sex on my mind. You know how some people order salad with dressing? I order mine nude.

I just read a fascinating statistic—that last year 3000 chastity belts were sold in this country—and 22,000 keys.

I'm very tense and nervous about things like sex. I once bought a marriage manual and tried to perform the copyright notice.

I've had a complex ever since our wedding night when my wife told me to close my eyes, she wanted to slip into something more comfortable—and it was another hotel.

I used to know a girl named Shirley and she was wild. Really wild. She used to charge $20 for the key to her room. Not to get in, to get out!

Frustration is when a girl gives you the key to her room—and it's in the Y.W.C.A.

Ecstasy is what you get from a misprint in a sex manual.

I put a mattress and two pillows on top of my color television set. And the next time a girl finishes dinner and asks, "What's good on TV?"——

I just heard the craziest thing—a girl saying to a boy, "Is that all you ever think about?" What made it so crazy, they were rabbits.

I don't want to say anything about my love life but sometimes I get the feeling that Congress is running it.

My love life hasn't been the same since they spilled tenderizer on me at that nudist picnic.

Sexual equality is creating all kinds of interesting new problems. I know a girl who's pregnant and she isn't sure it's hers.

It doesn't make sense, like the headline: IMPOTENCE IS ON THE RISE.

RELATIVES

I'm beginning to wonder about my wife. Last night I said we hadn't had relations for three weeks—so she invited six of them over for dinner.

The city set up a Human Relations Department and I was their first customer. I wanted to find out if any of mine are.

My brother-in-law is coming to visit us and I'm getting ready for it. I spent a quiet weekend picking the letters out of our WELCOME mat.

My brother-in-law isn't really lazy. There just isn't too much demand for his line of work. He sells army coffee at orgies.

I come from a very poor background. You know how some people have a family tree? We had a family bush!

RELIGION

Every once in a while I like to think deep thoughts—like what does Jerry Falwell say when he stubs his toe?

Last night I got the ultimate rejection. I was in church praying for divine help and a deep majestic voice answered, "Take two aspirin and call Me in the morning."

If they allow women to become priests, who knows where it will lead? I can see it now. The number-one song on the 1984 Hit Parade: "You'd Be a Pip of a Pope!"

This morning I saw two priests meet on the street and one said, "I'm Brother Vincent. Haven't we met before?" And the other priest said, "I don't remember the name but the faith is familiar."

Our neighbor used to be a tour guide in the Vatican until that fateful day the Pope walked in and he said, "Speak of the Devil!"

I have a tip for members of the National Association of Manufacturers. Hire ministers. They work to beat hell!

I never realized what a hard job it was to be a minister until I saw this ad: WANTED—MINISTER TO BE SPIRITUAL LEADER TO A SMALL STRUGGLING CHURCH. MUST BE CAPABLE OF GIVING INSPIRATIONAL SERMONS, EFFECTIVE COUNSELING, BUILDING MEMBERSHIP, RAISING FUNDS, AND PROVIDING PARISHIONERS WITH THE KEY TO HAPPY AND SUCCESSFUL LIVING. LIGHT TYPING HELPFUL.

One of the first things you learn in a Christian Science church is, no matter what happens, never ask, "Is there a doctor in the house?"

It's really embarrassing at the end of a Billy Graham meeting, when he asks all the sinners who want to be saved to come to the front of the hall—and they direct you to the express lane.

We are all here to do the Lord's work. All except the atheists. They're on welfare.

This is a very important time of the year for religion. It's when non-church members have to be introduced to religion and many church members have to be introduced to their minister.

All of the major religions are losing members, which is embarrassing. Somehow I never figured the Army of the Lord would need a draft.

People seem to have lost a feeling for religion. Nowadays if you hear somebody speaking with reverence about the Last Supper, chances are they're on a diet.

You can always tell Judas in a painting of the Last Supper. He's the one asking for separate checks.

It's interesting how they're trying to make religion relevant to today's youth. For instance, they now have a version of the Garden of Eden story just for teenagers. The snake tempts Eve with a pizza!

I'm toying with the idea of starting a new religion for people who have really had it. It'll be called THE FIRST CHURCH OF THE LAST STRAW.

I go to a church that's so liberal, it's only open on Tuesdays.

Personally, I believe in the hereafter. What I find hard to believe in is the here and now!

RESORTS

I spent the weekend at the world's dullest resort. Really. If you think there's no life on Mars, you should see this place.

It's a very quiet resort. Nothing much happens during the day, but at night all hell breaks loose. Everybody sits around the candy machine and watches the chocolate bars melt.

It's a wonderful resort. They're doing something every minute. I think it's the guests.

One day the swimming instructor was sick so they sent over the golf pro. I almost drowned. He kept telling me to keep my head down.

RESTAURANTS

I go to a very honest smorgasbord restaurant. They have a sign saying: ALL YOU CAN EAT FOR $2.98! If you go back for seconds, the manager stops you. He says, "That's all you can eat for $2.98!"

What a vacation. We spent $200 just getting gas. You can't believe those restaurants!

I go to one of those old-fashioned restaurants where they give you all the salad you can make, all the bread you can eat, all the beer you can drink, and all the bill you can pay.

I can't help it. When I go into a restaurant, I always read the menu from right to left. Yesterday I had the most delicious $4.95 I ever tasted.

And the prices! Remember when restaurants had signs saying: WATCH YOUR HAT AND COAT? Now they have signs saying: FORGET YOUR HAT AND COAT. WATCH YOUR STEAK!

I'm fascinated by those fancy restaurants where they cook a thin slice of beef over a Sterno stove and charge you $15. I think it's called Steak Flim-Flambé.

If there's one thing I hate, it's eating in one of those restaurants that cater to shoppers. You know the kind—where seven-layer cake is an entree.

Where, if you order steak, they have to send out for it.

Everything is on the sweet side. You ever drink a martini with a marshmallow in it?

And the portions are very small. I once had a five-course meal in one of these restaurants—and as I was leaving the hostess said, "You must have dinner with us again sometime." I said, "Great! How about now?"

And you see a lot of phonies at restaurants. You really do. I mean, who asks for the wine list at McDonald's?

We stopped in one place that offered a blue plate special. One plate and that's what you turn!

It's one of those restaurants that always serves pumpernickel because it's tasty, nutritious and doesn't show the dirt.

I'd like to send my compliments to the chef. It's the first time I was ever served roast beef, coffee and ice cream—all at the same temperature.

I'm not saying the food in this restaurant is bad. I'm just saying that people who eat there get the Tums rush!

And I'd also like to say something about the service during dinner. I didn't know the post office catered.

It's one of those friendly restaurants. The waiter said, "Would you like some Warm Duck?" I said, "You mean Cold Duck. You don't know your wines." He said, "Warm Duck. You don't know our refrigerator."

I said to the waiter, "I'll have a dozen oysters." He said, "Oysters aren't at their peak." I said, "Neither am I. That's why I want a dozen of them!"

You know what has always bugged me about restaurants? When they give you a basket with six rolls, eight slices of bread, forty-two crackers and one pat of butter! It's ridiculous. I use more butter than that on a burned finger!

RETIREMENT

Retirement is when your take-home pay makes the trip on its own.

This is a very economical year to be retired. By the time you figure out what you can afford for breakfast, it's lunch!

Retirement is when, every year, your blood pressure gets higher and your bank balance gets lower.

You can always tell the guest of honor at a retirement dinner. He's the only one who yawns after the boss's favorite joke.

A retirement dinner has been defined as the very last opportunity an employee has to be fed up by the company.

A retirement dinner is where management gives the guest of honor a solid gold watch case and the pension plan gives him the works.

I know a fella who's retiring after fifty years with a company and it's just great. When he started, he made $5.00 a week and all he could afford was a cold-water furnished room and onion sandwiches. But he worked and sweated and got promotions and gave everything he had to his job, and so now, after fifty years, in 1983, he's retiring with a $12,000 pension— and all he'll be able to afford is a cold-water furnished room and onion sandwiches.

A retirement dinner is where the foreman says, "John Jones will be leaving us after fifty-three years of faithful service, but he'll always be with us in our memories." And the boss says to the personnel manager, "Who?"

For the last six years I've been getting memos from THE DESK OF JOE JONES. Last month Joe Jones retired and I'm really broken up. I never cared too much for Jones—but his desk I really miss.

Retirement is the snapdragon period of our lives. Part of us has lost its snap and the rest is dragon.

ROASTS

What can you really say about (TOASTMASTER)? He's all bull and a yard wide!

Now if you'll just pull up a couple of chairs and sit down, I'd like to begin.

You've just been listening to that famous Chinese toastmaster, On Too Long!

(TOASTMASTER), I don't quite know how to put this—but you're giving dullness a bad name.

I never met our toastmaster before but the last speaker told me how to recognize him. He said, "If you see two people talking and one of them is yawning—he's the other one!"

REPLY TO A ROASTING: I want to thank you for this wonderful evening. You've made me feel right at home—which will give you some idea what kind of a marriage I have.

Some people don't know what's cooking. You don't even have a recipe!

People tell me you stand out from the crowd. Who do you hang out with—the Seven Dwarfs?

I like that outfit. I didn't know they made plaid tuxedos.

I was watching him during dinner. Eat? If he were Chinese he'd use three chopsticks!

I couldn't look up to him if he wore platform shoes.

He reminds me of those great figures of Washington, Jefferson, Lincoln and Teddy Roosevelt on Mount Rushmore. He's not famous and he's not a President. He just has a head like a rock.

Doesn't _____ have an interesting face? His biggest problem is, if he stops anybody on a dark, quiet street to ask the time, they always give him their wallet!

_____'s face looks like his hobby is stepping on rakes.

Aren't they a lovely couple? They remind me of psychotherapy. She's therapy.

Gutsy? Who else do you know wears a factory-second pacemaker?

Dull? Every day he talks to his plants and it's a heartrending sight. You ever see a geranium yawn?

Some people are painstaking. He is painsgiving.

He thinks small. He's the type who'd chop down a sequoia to make toothpicks.

I wouldn't call him a liar. Let's just say he lives on the wrong side of the facts.

If he ever tried to walk the straight and narrow, he'd need a safety net!

He puts his foot in his mouth so often, his favorite flavor is toe.

Let's not say he's an obstructionist. Let's just say he's solution pollution!

Conceited? He can take three bows on a waiter hitting a ketchup bottle.

Dumb? If you gave him a penny for his thoughts, you'd have change coming.

Eat? One time I took her to a Chinese restaurant, gave her chopsticks and she started two fires!

When it comes to body language, she has a vocabulary you can't believe!

But you have to give her credit. She never gives up. She's now on the twenty-third year of her 14-day Beauty Plan!

RUSSIA

Disneyland is made up of fantasy, fairy tales and make-believe. The Russians have the same thing. They're called elections.

I never felt sorry for the Russians until I read that _____ is the secretary of the Communist Party. Have you seen his legs?

Getting affectionate in Russia must be a problem. I mean, how does that sound—Comrade Pussycat?

SALESMEN

Our sales manager is getting a little discouraged. He says what this world really needs is a jumper cable that works on salesmen.

I had an interesting talk with two salesmen at this convention. One salesman was saying that his boss thought so much of him, he placed a chauffeur-driven limousine at his disposal and told the business manager never to question any item on this particular salesman's expense account. I said, "Incredible!" The second salesman said, "That's nothing. My boss thinks so much of me, when I had an argument with our biggest customer, he canceled their account and gave me a $10,000 bonus to make up for the loss in my commission!" I said, "Incredible!" Then the two salesmen turned to me and asked, "What has your boss done for you?" I said, "Well, he did send me to charm school." They said, "Charm school? What could charm school teach a man in your position?" I said, "A great deal. For instance, I now say 'Incredible' instead of 'Bull!'"

A good salesman is always trying to get an edge in wordwise.

Hens make money while sitting down. Salesmen don't!

Is this man a salesman? He's had his foot in so many doors, they show him on floor plans.

When we hire a new salesman, we always use the ink-blot test. We show each applicant an ink blot and the first one who tries to sell us a new pen gets the job.

Is this man a salesman? Yesterday he sold me four new tires I didn't need. What makes it even worse, I have a motorcycle.

Contact our Sales Department—when you care enough to vend the very best.

Expect no good to come of any day that starts off with the boss saying, "You're a salesman? You couldn't sell a fire extinguisher to Joan of Arc!"

Did you ever get the feeling your sales pitch is 0 and 3?

Ralph Nader keeps investigating things that don't work. No use talking. I've got to introduce him to our Sales Department.

It's like I told our Sales Department today: "Gentlemen, DO NOT OPEN UNTIL CHRISTMAS is great for presents. For order books, not so good!"

One time somebody painted a picture of our Sales Department. It was a still life.

Do you ever get the feeling your Sales Department couldn't sell Windex to a Peeping Tom?

This is the time of year when it's tough to be a salesman. The company wants results and the I.R.S. wants receipts.

The trouble with putting salesmen on a starting salary is, sometimes the salary starts but they don't!

We have the greatest deterrent ever when it comes to door-to-door salesmen. It's a sign on the front door that reads: POOR SPOKEN HERE.

SCHOOL

My wife is mad at me because I spent $200 on my daughter's graduation dress. Here's the way I look at it: how many times does a kid go from nursery school to kindergarten?

Tell me, when your kids come home from school and you ask them what they learned that day, do you ever get the feeling they're majoring in shrugging?

If you think Old Man River don't know nothin'—try talking to the kids in progressive schools!

I asked my son's history professor how he was doing and he

just shook his head. He said, "Mr. Orben, your son doesn't know his past from his elbow."

I try to talk to my kids in terms they understand. I tell them that going to school is like a potato chip in the cheese dip of life. It's a means to an end.

My ten-year-old had to take up a musical instrument for the school band and it's really added a new dimension to our home life. You ever hear Cole Porter played on a bass drum?

SCHOOL BUSES

I know a school bus driver whose favorite food is Jell-O. He loves to see something that's more nervous than he is.

What can you really say about a school bus driver who gets married? Some people just dig aggravation.

Kids today don't want to do anything that requires work. You think I'm kidding? Twenty of them just signed a petition to lower the first step on the school bus!

Now I know why school buses are yellow. Have you ever taken a good look at what they have to carry?

There's nothing bothering the average parent that couldn't be cured by making school buses one way.

SCHOOL VACATION

We've had our three kids home from school since June 29th and I think it's beginning to tell on my wife. Yesterday I asked her what time it was. She said, "Half past summer."

Each year our kids get nine weeks of summer vacation and

each year it always seems to go this way: The first three weeks my wife and I look for things we can all do together. The second three weeks we look for things the kids can do by themselves. And the last three weeks we look for loopholes in their birth certificates.

We didn't send our kids to camp for the summer and I think it's beginning to tell on my wife. Yesterday she went over to our neighborhood school, patted the front door and said, "Soon!"

SEX EDUCATION

I had a very sheltered youth. I was eighteen before they let me have a full-length mirror in the bathroom.

They're starting sex education way too young. You can tell. I just heard a kid saying, "Your crib or mine?"

You know something's terribly wrong when you see two kids playing strip hopscotch!

Did you hear about the two kids who came out of their first sex education class? One turned to the other and said, "I don't know about you, but as far as I'm concerned, Sesame Street has had it!"

You can always tell the bright kids from the dumb kids in sex education classes. The bright kids are promoted. The dumb kids are pregnant.

A sex education class is where almost everybody graduates magna cum lewder.

I can remember when a kid got married to learn about sex. Now they learn about sex so they won't have to get married.

I'll never forget the first time they told me about the birds and the bees. The next day a bee stung me and I started to cry. The teacher said, "What's the matter?" I said, "Don't touch me! I'm expecting!"

When I was a kid, the biggest step toward sex education was getting your own car. . . . Remember? If you had your own car, foreplay was putting it in neutral.

And it was very important to get the right size car. I once parked with a girl in a Volkswagen and I'll never forget what happened—nothing!

SHOPPING

A department store has given up carrying alarm clocks for a very simple reason. The way things are going, who can sleep?

So this woman standing with an armful of merchandise in a downtown department store suddenly starts to yell: "RAPE! RAPE!" Six clerks and a floorwalker rush over asking, "What happened?" She said, "Nothing happened." They said, "Then why did you yell 'RAPE'?" She said, "If I yelled 'SALESCLERK,' would you have come?"

I'm a little suspicious of our local liquor store. For instance, I didn't know you could get a first-growth Bordeaux that's lemon-flavored.

You don't know what it's like to be married to a vegetarian. Yesterday she ordered a case of Yoghurteater Gin!

My home town isn't very sophisticated. You can tell that from the supermarket. Where else do you have to go into the Gourmet Department to buy lard?

SHORTAGES

Shortages are when our cup runneth under.

All these shortages are really upsetting. My brother-in-law is so confused, yesterday he went to work.

If you're a gourmet, a meat shortage creates all kinds of problems. Like, what wine do you serve with Wheaties?

It's been so cold this year, there's already a shortage of sweaters. A haberdasher was trying to sell me one for $125. He said, "Sure the price is a little high but it's made from a very rare wool that can only be found on a special breed of sheep whose native habitat is the most inaccessible and remote reaches of the Himalayan Mountains. It's a beautiful yarn." I said, "And you tell it well."

SHOW BUSINESS

Being in show business is like this: the happiest day of your life can be the one in which four things happen—World War III is declared, the stock market crashes, a tidal wave destroys New York, and you get your first Las Vegas booking.

We had an interesting show last week. We had one act who was really offbeat. Unfortunately, he was a singer.

But I do have to admit, Dolly Parton has caused a little dissension in our home. My wife always gets suspicious of any singer I have to put my glasses on to hear.

And I was the first one to spot the fantastic talent of Barbra Streisand. I can remember taking Barbra Streisand into the biggest booking agency in America and just before we went into the agent's office I said, "This is it, Barbra, your big chance. This could lead to movies, Broadway, television, stardom. Don't let me down, Barbra. Go in there and dance like you've never danced before!"

They're trying to keep this quiet but a very popular singer who's getting on in years just had an emergency operation. They put in support tonsils.

It's really sad. After all these years, everything has gone limp on him. This is the only man I know who has to eat oysters just to snap his fingers.

People make a big thing out of yodeling but it's the most natural thing in the world. You wear leather shorts on a cold winter's morning and you'd yodel too!

A lot of performers complain about their agents but not me. I've got the world's greatest agent. He could sell Marcel Marceau to radio!

My agent doesn't miss a trick. Last week he tried to get 10% on an act of God.

I'm getting very discouraged. It's like I keep telling my agent: "If life is a cabaret, old chum, how come I ain't working?"

I don't want to complain, but my press agent couldn't get Robert E. Lee mentioned in *Gone With the Wind*.

I keep telling my agent I have one goal in life—to be booked into a town and when I go down to the Automobile Club to get a Triptik, they don't say, "Where?"

I played in one town that's so small, the First National Bank is a fella with big pockets.

AUDIENCE: You've just been great and I really appreciate it. We had an audience last night—sixty minutes of heavy breathing. Sounded like a group obscene phone call.

I always feel sorry for the audience at talk shows. The only thing they can do to express themselves is laugh or applaud—and that isn't too wide a range of communication. I can remember one talk show in which the announcer came out, held up his hand and said, "Ladies and gentlemen, don't panic—but the studio is on fire and I would like you all to get up and quietly leave the building." Two people got up and the rest clapped.

Nothing makes a stripper grow moodier
Than seeing the act after her get nudier.

Believe me, it isn't easy making TV commercials. Take Mrs. Olson, that nice lady who spends all of her time in other people's kitchens drinking coffee. Easy job? Forget it! Hasn't slept in fourteen years! . . . All night long she watches Charlie Chan movies on the Late Show. She isn't too thrilled with the movies but she digs anyone who drinks tea!

Talent will out. Actually, mine outed about ten years ago and never came back.

Last night I saw a play that was so sick, at intermission they didn't serve orange juice—they served chicken soup!

The nice part about being in X-rated movies, when you get up in the morning, you're dressed for work.

SINGLES

Now there's a singles bar in Sun City. It's for people who aren't getting any younger.

You can always tell a swinging singles resort by the sign they have in the lobby: CHASTE MAKES WASTE!

I just heard about the saddest thing—a singles cemetery.

SMALL TOWNS

I come from a town that's so small, we didn't even have crime in the streets. Well, let me clarify that. We had crime. What we didn't have is streets.

I had some bad news from my home town. The symphony orchestra had to cancel its performance of Beethoven's Fifth. The fella who played first ukulele quit.

I was telling my wife how backward the town is. They even voted for Calvin Coolidge. She said, "Lots of people voted for Calvin Coolidge." I said, "Last year?"

Did you hear about the small-town doctor who's also the mortician? He specializes in eye, ear, nose and croak.

This town is so dull, they used to print the newspaper three weeks in advance.

This town is so dull, the local newspaper changed the name of the OBITUARY column. It's now known as WHAT TO DO ON SATURDAY NIGHT.

This town was so poor, the fat lady in the circus weighed 135 pounds.

This town was so poor, we didn't even have grain elevators. We had grain stairways.

SNOW

How 'bout this weather? Do you realize this is the first snow job in weeks that hasn't come from Washington?

I'll tell you how bad the weather has been. Yesterday I was mugged for my snow shovel.

Do you know they even have a special curse for this kind of weather? "May you have a bad back, a big shovel and wet snow!"

If you're fat, middle-aged and out of shape, it's very smart to shovel two feet of snow off your walk. How else are they going to get the stretcher up from the ambulance?

Remember when kids used to pick up extra money clearing sidewalks? Now you hand them a snow shovel and they want to know where to plug it in.

I used to put snow tires on my car, but they're no good. They melt!

SOAP OPERAS

My wife loves soap operas. Last night I came home and I said, "What's new?" She said, "Well, Janie had an abortion; Sam's business went bankrupt; Laura's husband ran away with a belly dancer; little Johnny is in jail for smoking pot; Grandfather Adams' house burned down; Sis won't be able to graduate from public school because she's pregnant; and Brother was caught stripping the tires from a police car." I said, "That's incredible. What's the program called?" She said, "*Life Can Be Beautiful.*"

They say that the people in soap operas are just like the people next door. I believe it. I live next to a massage parlor.

In every soap opera there's a scheming woman who is trying to steal good Dr. Bob away from his faithful wife, Bess. And they have some pretty far-out scheming women. I saw one with an overbite. But I mean, an overbite! In fact, that's how faithful wife Bess started to get suspicious. One night good Dr. Bob came home with four nostrils!

You should have seen this kid's teeth. When she said, "Kiss me, you fool!"—she wasn't kidding.

You couldn't blame Dr. Bob for being fascinated. Name me one other woman who can eat corn on the cob through a venetian blind!

And in every soap opera there's somebody called Cyril Sly who's trying to cheat Grandma Perkins out of her life savings. They want her to invest it in a questionable business. I think it's questionable. They're going to make power zippers for wealthy exhibitionists.

Lately soap operas have been going in for more daring themes. For instance, they're implying that Sister Sue might have V.D. They don't come right out and say she has V.D. But yesterday when she blew a kiss to the family—everybody ducked!

And they really drag these soap operas out. I saw one where Cousin Mildred was pregnant for eighty-three months. This was the first time in history a kid was ever born and went straight from the delivery room to high school!

I've often thought that if the *Titanic* had been a soap opera it'd still be sinking.

SOCIAL SECURITY

Social Security is a little like putting quarters into a nickel slot machine.

People on Social Security have a real problem for Lent. What more is there to give up?

Social Security is what keeps you going in your old age. I thought it was prunes.

If you're retired, Social Security is like seeing the minister's wife in a low-cut gown. It's not much but you can't look down on it.

I counted on Social Security
To buy food and clothing and trips.
So now I'm on Social Security—
Mostly I use it for tips!

I know it's fashionable to put down Social Security, but I have an uncle who gets $2000 a month from Social Security—and that's not bad. On the third of every month he sells 2000 raffle tickets for $1.00 each. What does the winner get? His Social Security check!

SONS

My wife says our son is having an identity crisis. I said, "An identity crisis? So get him bigger name tapes!"

Kids are really amazing. Like my neighbor's son. All day long he lays in bed with a bottle in his mouth, burping. What makes it so amazing—he's thirty-four!

ABOUT SOMEONE WITH A BEARD: Do you realize that just fifteen years ago his father was calling him a little shaver?

I have only two things to ask of my son: to start growing up and to stop growing hair.

The Weather Bureau forecast hazardous driving conditions. I don't know if that means a snowstorm or my son has the car.

My son spent his vacation at home, working—me, his mother, his grandparents.

Scientists are desperately trying to put the sun to work. So are millions of parents.

I asked my son if he could go around corners on two wheels. He said, "Sure." I said, "There's the lawnmower."

My son has devoted this summer to the elimination of world hunger, poverty, prejudice, illiteracy and two or three persistent pimples.

SPEAKERS

As toastmaster, I'll try to keep my part of the program to a minimum. Which isn't easy. You see, every toastmaster feels like a eunuch in a harem. He'd like to be the main attraction only he's not cut out for it.

The most difficult thing a speaker has to learn is not to nod while the toastmaster is praising him.

Behind every successful speaker there's a Program Chairman —praying he is.

We once had a speaker who was so bad, three empty seats asked for their money back!

There are two rules that every speaker should observe: never drink on an empty stomach—and never speak on an empty head.

Always remember the first rule of public speaking: be brief— no matter how long it takes you to do it!

I gave a talk at one club that has a very sneaky way of keeping their speeches short. They don't have water on the speaker's stand—prune juice!

I'm going to hold this speech to fifteen minutes. Frankly, I've never talked longer than fifteen minutes since the time I overheard two people discussing me during a speech. One said,

"He's pretty tall, isn't he?" And the other said, "Yes. Hot air rises!"

Our club seems to specialize in Road to Mandalay speakers. Before they're halfway through, the yawns come up like thunder.

You know you've talked too long when time is running out and so is your audience.

A time limit is a compass for people who wander off the topic.

Every speaker has a mouth;
An arrangement rather neat.
Sometimes it's filled with wisdom.
Sometimes it's filled with feet.

I always make it a point to speak grammatically. Who knows? It might become popular again.

I get very nervous in front of audiences. Very nervous. I once rehearsed for two weeks just to deliver a silent prayer.

If you're a public speaker, to err, err, err, err is human.

As anyone who ever tried to hire a lecturer knows—talk is steep!

I don't want to brag, but you know how some people get a standing ovation? I get a kneeling ovation!

SPEAKERS' "AD-LIBS"

I wanted to start off this evening with a bang but the parking lot attendant beat me to it.

This is a very special night for our parking lot attendant. It's the tenth anniversary of his learner's permit.

Before I begin, I've been asked to make this announcement: There's a blue 1978 Buick in the parking lot with the headlights on and the radio playing. Would the owner please see the parking lot attendant? They're going to hold a memorial service for your battery.

I'm standing up here with butterflies in my stomach. I'm not nervous. My wife just has some weird recipes.

I won't say what I'm doing up here, but my whole life is passing before my eyes.

AFTER A SPEAKER WHO WAS ON TOO LONG: I'm sure we could all listen to _____ forever. And I think we have.

AFTER AN OFF-COLOR JOKE: So that's what you want! I don't know how to tell you this—but you're under arrest!

AFTER AN OUTRAGEOUS PUN: Now you know what causes the loneliness of the long-distance punner.

AFTER YOUR FIRST LAUGH: This is my barbecue speech. It takes a little time to get started, but I'm hot now!

AS YOU PUT ON GLASSES: Some people put on glasses to help them look intellectual. Some people put on glasses to help them look sincere. Some people put on glasses to help them look studious. Personally, I just put on glasses to help me look.

DEBATE: Sir, try to keep your words as sweet as possible. Before this evening is over, you may have to swallow them.

DELAYED REACTION: That's one of those Polaroid jokes. It takes about a minute to get the whole picture.

DURING A DISCUSSION: Have you noticed something? Trying to pin him down is like trying to smooth out a water bed.

DURING A DISCUSSION: Let's try to keep this on the subject. I'd rather adjourn at ten o'clock sharp than twelve o'clock dull.

FOLLOW-UP TO YOUR FIRST BIG JOKE AFTER A QUIET START: I'm like the post office. I'm slow but I eventually deliver.

IF YOU'RE WEARING TAILS: Isn't this something? I just got an obscene phone call from a penguin!

NO LAUGHS: This is my corduroy routine. One straight line after another.

By this time you're probably wondering what I do for a living.

I have only two problems tonight. This tuxedo isn't mine—and these jokes are.

OPENING FOR RAINY WEATHER: I don't know about you, but I'm building an ark.

WHEN A JOKE DIES: This program is coming to you live—all except that joke.

WHEN A JOKE DIES: That went over like a nude beach in Siberia.

WHEN SOMEONE TOPS YOU: Did you ever get the feeling you're standing on the *Titanic* and Mark Spitz just borrowed your life belt?

WHEN SOMEONE TOPS YOU IN AN EXCHANGE: You know something, at this very moment, I'd give anything if I had another line—of work!

WHEN SOMEONE ON YOUR STAFF TOPS YOU: That was ——————, one of the funniest former sales managers we've ever had.

WHEN YOU CONCEDE A DEFEAT, LOWER THE MICROPHONE AND SAY: I'll have to lower this. After that vote, I'm not as big around here as I used to be.

WHEN YOU GARBLE WORDING: I haven't heard anything like that since I tried to read a bowl of alphabet soup!

SPEAKERS' COMMENTS

Before we begin, I want you to know how impressed I am by this august body. I was standing outside during the cocktail hour and it's the first time I ever saw a group drinking factory-whistle style. One blast after another!

OPENING: My name is _____, your friendly neighborhood sex object.

WHEN PRESENTED WITH AN AWARD: I want to thank you all for this very great honor. It's so good to know that through all these years my mirror and I haven't been wrong.

SPEECH FOLLOW-UP: I always enjoy one of _____'s speeches. They're like a big red balloon—99% hot air but beautifully packaged!

REPEAT ENGAGEMENT: I want to thank the committee for asking me here again—particularly in this warm weather. Usually they want me back in the winter. For instance, last week I finished a speech and the program chairman asked me if I was available in January. Well, he didn't exactly use those words. He just said it'll be a cold day when they see me again!

I understand that, in the past, this town suffered very extensively from wind damage. Nevertheless, I'm still going to do this speech.

Before I begin, I must say how impressed I am by the integrity and conscientiousness and honesty of the speakers on this program. One of the speakers told me that last night he met this gorgeous redhead in the lobby. They had dinner together, a few drinks, then they went up to his room and, before anything else happened, he gave his speech. I said, "That's incredible. To think that at a time like that you'd practice your speech." He said, "Well, I never lie to my wife." I said,

"What's your wife got to do with it?" He said, "I told her I was speaking before an affair in the (NAME OF HOTEL)."

I'll try to keep this short. I've found that most speeches are like salt water taffy. The more they're drawn out, the thinner they get.

I'll try to keep this short. Every time I see one of those signs that say: WHERE WILL YOU SPEND ETERNITY?—I think of some speeches I've sat through.

It's an interesting feeling talking to an audience in which 90% of the people know more about the subject than you do. It's like playing Russian roulette with a machine gun.

Why is everybody sitting in the back? If ideas are contagious, you're never gonna catch any back there!

I don't want to seem immodest, but my name on a program does get some attention. After this speech was listed in the bulletin, your program chairman told me he received a letter. It said: "Dear Mr. _____: I read that (YOUR NAME) is going to be the principal speaker at the next meeting and you're also starting a membership drive. Tell me, is the drive in or out?"

I don't want to brag, but (CELEBRITY) and I get the same lecture fee—ten, zero, zero, zero dollars. Unfortunately, mine comes with a decimal point.

I want to congratulate you on your Finance Committee. This is a rented tuxedo. And you don't know what it does to a speaker to know his tuxedo is getting $5.00 an hour and he's getting a buck and a half!

You can tell it's a rented tuxedo. Have you ever seen such a fit? Looks more like a convulsion!

I always try to remember the A.B.C. of good public speaking

—Always Be Cheerful. And before going out to face an audience, I also try to remember the X.Y.Z. of good public speaking—Examine Your Zipper!

You know what I like about this organization? The members are so honest. The last time I was here, I finished my talk and as I was leaving the hall I bumped into a member coming in late. I said, "Did you miss my speech?" She said, "Not a bit!"

By now, you're probably wondering why the prayer was silent and I'm not.

Please! Don't tell me I'm going to rise to the occasion. Just give me more yeast.

What I'm doing is called a "monologue." For those of you who are unfamiliar with the term, a monologue is a conversation between Howard Cosell and anybody.

The program director really wasn't too sure how I'd do tonight. I asked him the capacity of this room. He said, "It sleeps 300."

AFTER APPLAUSE: Really, was I that good or are you just trying to keep your hands warm?

SPEAKERS' PROBLEMS

AFTER A LONG INTRODUCTION: I'd like to make a few brief remarks tonight. For those of you who aren't familiar with the term "brief remarks," it's what you have time for after _____ introduces you.

HOT MEETING ROOM: I want to congratulate the management of this hotel on the air conditioning. Frankly, I've never seen air in such condition!

HOT MEETING ROOM: Incidentally, after the meeting we have an extra treat for you. We're all going to get together and toast marshmallows over the air conditioner.

LOUD TALKER: Sir, could you keep it down? You're shaking up some of the audience and waking up the rest.

SLAM BOTH OF YOUR PALMS TOGETHER WHEN BOTHERED BY A FLY OR A MOTH: If that was a member, I'm sorry!

WHEN ADJUSTING THE MICROPHONE AT A FUND-RAISING AFFAIR: This reminds me of some pledges I've seen. It's mighty hard to raise.

WHEN SOMEONE COMES INTO A VERY LARGE AUDIENCE LATE: Come in. We've just started. Is there anybody here you don't know?

WHEN THINGS ARE GETTING OUT OF HAND: Wait a minute! As they say in massage parlors, "Hold everything!"

WHEN YOU COMMIT A FAUX PAS: If you'll just wait a moment, I have to get something out of my mouth. A foot!

WHEN YOU FIDDLE WITH A MIKE THAT ISN'T WORKING PROPERLY: This is one of those pharmaceutical mikes. You have to shake well before using.

WHEN YOU GET CONFUSED: As you can see, I have a wonderful way of making a long story short. I can't read my notes.

WHEN YOU INTRODUCE SOMEONE WHO ISN'T IN THE AUDIENCE: That's the trouble with people who have get-up-and-go. They get up and go.

WHEN YOU LOSE YOUR PLACE: I haven't been this confused since I tried to find the men's room at Women's Lib.

WHEN YOU'RE ASKED A VERY LONG QUESTION: Sir, as they say at circumcisions, could you cut this short?

WHEN YOU'RE HAVING TROUBLE ADJUSTING THE MICROPHONE: You have to be very careful what you say while doing this. One time I was having trouble with the microphone and I said, "Can anybody tell me what to do with this?" They did.

WHEN YOU'RE TRYING TO REMEMBER SOMETHING: Isn't this awful? Every year Detroit is recalling more and I'm recalling less.

SPEECHES

Humor in public speaking is a little like silicone. It can take something that's flat and turn it into something outstanding.

The first thing you have to do with a speech is make sure it's understandable to even the world's dumbest person. Show it to your brother-in-law.

I don't want to seem immodest, but last week I finished a speech and the program chairman came up to me and said I really rang the bell. Well, he didn't exactly use those words. He just said I was the biggest ding-a-ling he ever heard.

You know how millions of Americans have turned down their thermostats to save on heat? Well, I've tried to do the same thing with this speech—and I think I've succeeded. You'd be surprised how many people come up and tell me it's not so hot.

Cutting your speech by 50% is half the prattle!

You always have to be careful of little old ladies after a speech because they don't kid around. One time I finished a rather long talk and this sweet little thing came up to me, put a gloved hand into mine and said, "Mr. Orben, has anyone ever told you you're a fascinating speaker?" I said, "No. No one ever has." She said, "Then whatever gave you the idea?"

If you don't mind, I'm going to read this speech. Some people have a good memory; they're glib, eloquent. Me, I couldn't ad-lib a "Whoopee!" at a New Year's Eve party!

When it comes to trash compactors, you just can't beat a five-minute limit on speeches.

I started giving shorter speeches the day I overheard two members of my audience talking. One said, "He's not as big a bore as he used to be." And the other answered, "No, I think he's lost weight!"

SPORTS

So many sports events are being shown on TV, yesterday Howard Cosell called up the Mayo Clinic and said, "Doc, can a tongue get a hernia?"

Do you realize that, if God were Howard Cosell, Moses would have had to send down for more tablets?

Every time it snows, I go cross-country skiing. I have bad brakes and bald tires.

Before you can go skiing, you have to wax all the surfaces that come in contact with the snow. With me that's easy. I just get out the jar of wax and sit in it!

Skiing doesn't make sense. Girls save their money for months to go to a ski resort to have fun—and the first thing the instructor tells them is to keep their knees together.

I was at a bowling alley and I heard these two women talking. One said, "Lucille, last night I came the closest I've ever come to bowling a perfect 300 game!" Her friend said, "That's fantastic! What did you bowl?" She said, "Sixty-two!"

Happiness is a basketball coach who spends most of his time talking into players' knees.

I had a wonderful weekend. I was watching America's greatest comedy team—(CELLAR TEAM).

Do-it-yourself is a sky diver who only bails out over Forest Lawn!

Sky diving is a fascinating sport. When you make your first jump, if your parachute opens, they have something for you— a big bouquet of roses. And if your parachute doesn't open, they still have something for you—a spatula!

Sky diving is the only sport I know where, if you don't do it right, they have to dig you up and bury you!

And it's very easy to spot a chicken sky diver. When they leave the plane they jump up!

SPRING

Spring is God's way of saying: "One more time!"

We should all be thankful the government isn't in the season business. I'd hate for there not to be enough springtime to go round.

April is when you get that tremendous feeling of exhilaration that comes from finishing the last piece of Christmas fruit-cake!

April is when the couples who took separate vacations last August get their divorce.

I like June. I got married in June. I still like June.

June is the time of year when dry cleaners face their biggest challenge: how to get pizza stains out of a white prom jacket!

I love this time of the year. This morning I looked out at our window box and the flowers were so fresh, so beautifully formed, so rich in color—you could almost smell the plastic.

STOCKBROKERS

My broker is living proof of reincarnation. In a previous life he had to be ticket seller for the *Titanic!*

Brokers are always doing things to scare you. Like this morning he called me up and said: "Your stock has split!" I didn't even know it was defective!

Then there's the parking lot attendant who became a stockbroker. Now he dents pocketbooks.

Do you think this means something? This morning my broker came in wearing a crash helmet.

I gave my broker a Christmas present. It's for those special days when the market drops 30 points—gray flannel Pampers.

I don't want to criticize my broker's recommendations, but Wall Street just voted him the Man of the Year—1929!

This is no time for emotionalism, but I understand the recession has really hit stockbrokers. So have a few customers.

My broker is in a forty-story building. If you don't believe one, he tells you another.

My broker has really called the turns in the market. Six months after every major decline, he says: "There's another one!"

I don't want to be critical of my stockbroker but I think the last family he helped to financial success was the Waltons.

STOCK MARKET

I always get upset when I read about profit taking in the stock market—because I know whose profit they're taking.

THE STOCK MARKET IS AN EQUAL OPPORTUNITY DESTROYER.

Money is the root of all evil—and the stock market is Roto-Rooter.

I'm convinced my wife really doesn't listen to me. Last night I looked up from the paper and said, "I got burned in the stock market today." She said, "Wait, I'll get some butter."

My wife never lets me forget a mistake. Yesterday she gave me a nudge, pointed to one of those signs saying JESUS SAVES, and said, "You see that?" I said, "So?" She said, "And *you're* in the stock market!"

The way I see it, if God hadn't meant for us to be in the stock market He never would have given us migraines.

We have a very polite stock market these days. It keeps saying, "Pardon me for not rising."

I'm just glad the stock market closes on weekends. It gives my fingernails a chance to grow back.

December is when you hear a great deal about profit taking. Personally, I have firsthand knowledge of what profit taking is all about. Last year the stock market took mine and never brought it back.

So many people have been hurt by the stock market, they're beginning to call it the Ow Jones Average.

I subscribe to one of those stock advisory services. I won't say how many times they've been wrong but they're listed as a non-prophet organization.

They're the ones who accurately predicted the 1929 crash. Unfortunately, they predicted it last week.

They say the stock market is backing and filling. I don't know what it's filling but it sure ain't pockets!

I specialize in Hawaiian-type stocks. The minute I buy them, they go aloha!

They say you can't take it with you. I know. But the way things are going, I think my stocks are going to get there before I do!

Gold is something you find in the ground. So are my stocks.

Because of oil, the Arabs have most of their wealth in the ground. Because of the stock market, so do we!

Nowadays a market rally is like getting into an UP elevator on the *Titanic*.

My neighbor is so pessimistic about the stock market, he's studying speed reading just to be able to read the tape during a crash.

The saddest story I ever heard is about an investor who dropped a bundle in the stock market and went to an X-rated movie to forget his troubles. And in the very first scene the girl loses her shirt.

I'll tell you how I've been doing in the stock market. Yesterday I sent my broker a thank-you note—and all I did was break even!

Anyone who thinks there's safety in numbers has never looked at the stock market page.

Remember those signs saying: SAVE WATER. TAKE A SHOWER TOGETHER! I just saw one saying: INVEST IN THE STOCK MARKET. TAKE A BATH TOGETHER!

It's ridiculous. The stock market is now so low, it'd have to gain a hundred points just to crash!

The way the stock market is going, for the first time I truly understand why all new buildings have windows you can't open.

Sometimes I feel that all of us small investors are like a leaky faucet: a lot of little drips going down the drain.

Beware of any stock market report that starts off with: "It's four o'clock. Do you know where your profits are?"

Abraham Lincoln said you can't fool all of the people all of the time. Now if we could only convince the stock market.

I just wrote to the Securities and Exchange Commission. I have a few securities I wouldn't mind exchanging.

Investing in the stock market is a little like taking the pins out of a new shirt. No matter how carefully you do it, you're going to get stuck!

The stock market scene can make you uptight;
When it's down all day—I'm up all night!

At least you get a lot of exercise in the stock market. You run scared; you raise your hopes; and you push your luck!

One good thing about the stock market—even when it's going to hell, it always has a round-trip ticket.

You can tell that speculation is coming back into the market. I just got a tip on a company that's going to make a fortune. They rent hangers at orgies.

The stock market is booming again. The stock market—that's the businessman's Santa Anita!

I'm feeling as frisky as any young pup;
My broker just told me the market is up!

Basically, the stock market is on terra firma. It's a little more firma and there's a lot less terror.

STUPIDITY

If you wanted to brainwash him, you could use a thimble for a bucket.

My girl friend is always asking dumb questions. Yesterday I sat down on the couch beside her and reached to turn off the light. She said, "Are you going to conserve energy?" I said, "No. I'm going to give it everything I've got!"

If his I.Q. was any lower, he'd trip over it.

Dumb? He'd tell the Godfather, "Over my dead body!"

Dumb? He'd find a cure for nymphomania.

Dumb? He just bought a motorcycle with an air conditioner.

Dumb? How do you misspell I.O.U.?

SUMMER

A picnic is where you start worrying about strange things—like how many calories are in an ant?

I always enjoy picnics right up to the time I'm eating a cream cheese sandwich and I see one of the raisins start to move.

Summer is when you realize what this country really needs—a vegetarian mosquito.

I love the summertime. I did an open-air show the other night and the applause was deafening. Two people were applauding and the rest were swatting mosquitoes!

I know this may sound crazy, but I like mosquitoes. They're the only ones left who want me for my body.

July is when the teenagers who don't have enough money to go to Europe—go!

In this kind of weather there are only three ways to keep cool: wear light clothes, drink cold liquids, and spend all of your time in front of an air conditioner. Oh—one more thing. The air conditioner should be in Fairbanks, Alaska.

If you don't think this is the land of the free, just let your relatives know you have a summer cottage!

August is when your kids don't want to leave the summer camp they didn't want to go to in July.

SUMMER CAMP

Summer camps are places that are usually staffed by seventeen-year-old counselors—which is kind of interesting. You wouldn't trust them with your car—but your kids, okay!

I think it's about time to send the kids to summer camp. All day long my wife has been sewing names into their clothes— and you should see those names!

The first thing you do when sending children to a summer camp is sew name tapes into all their clothes. This is very important because then, at the end of the summer, ten other families will know who to thank for their kid's new wardrobe.

I always look forward to summer camp time. I'm one of those parents who find that school runs out just about the time my patience does.

Tell me, if family life is so great, why is it that when your wife says, "The kids are coming home from camp today"—you say, "Who?"

You can always tell the parents who have sent five kids away to summer camp. From force of habit they stand waiting outside of empty bathrooms.

I'll say one thing for the way they teach penmanship in schools these days: it's really great. When your kids write home from camp, you can't read a word!

Our kids have a great way of reassuring us. It's the first time I ever saw an "Everything is fine" card written in blood.

And summer camps are very expensive. Summer camps are where the kids wear shorts and the parents have them.

I'm writing a book about the Indian summer camp I'm sending my kid to. It's called *"Bury My Heart at Wounded Wallet."*

Do you know that some parents are spending as much as $1800 to send their kids away for the summer? Eighteen hundred dollars! I wouldn't pay $1800 if the camp was named David and the counselor was named Ronnie!

Summer camp is where parents pay $1800 so their kids can live in such a way that, if they were at home, they'd complain.

We have a real family crisis going on. My son wants to come home from summer camp—and we had to sell it to send him to summer camp.

My son came home from camp and I asked him what he learned during the summer. He said the counselor taught him how to answer a question with either "Yes, sir" or "No, sir." I said, "He did?" He said, "Yeah."

Summer camps are great because they teach kids to do things

with their hands. The first day they catch poison ivy and the rest of the summer they scratch!

But they do teach the kids useful arts and crafts. You should see what my son brought home last year. We're the only family on the block with a wrought-iron wineglass!

This glass is so heavy, if you lift it to drink to somebody's health—you lose your own!

I'm liberal and all that, but sometimes I worry about some of the things they permit at the summer camp we sent our kids to. Tell me, what's a conjugal visit?

There is only one effective way to handle the clothes your kid brings back from summer camp. First you put a disinfectant to them. Then you put a detergent to them. Then you put a bleach to them. And then you put a match to them!

My kid earned a black belt in karate and by the time the summer was over everything else matched!

When your kids come home from camp,
With their clothes be very cautious;
It's a sight you won't forget—
A washing machine getting nauseous!

SUMMER JOBS

April is when the boss's son gets the summer job your kids will be asking about in June.

When I was a kid I had a wonderful summer job. My mother paid me 25¢ an hour to stand on the sidewalk to make sure someone didn't come into the house—me!

Misery is a businessman with four nephews, three nieces, and one summer job.

The summer is when two million students look for part-time jobs. I know a boss who says he has plenty of part-time jobs—but he has full-time employees doing them!

My teenager got a summer job. He's a short-order cook in what used to be our favorite diner.

Summer jobs can be a very educational experience. My son is a senior in high school and during the summer he works as a busboy in a restaurant. And he's learned an awful lot from the other busboys. Why not? They're his teachers.

SUPERMARKETS

I didn't mind when our local supermarket put up a canopy and hired a doorman. I didn't even mind when they made you phone ahead for reservations. But when they put a meter on the shopping cart, that was going too far!

A senior citizen brought a small selection of groceries to the checkout counter of a supermarket and watched the clerk ring it up. Then the clerk handed him the register tape and he studied it for so long, she asked, "Is it right?" "Miss," he sighed, "it's correct. Right, no!"

I was on the checkout line at our supermarket and the girl handed me the tape. I couldn't believe it. I said, "Is this what I have to pay or is your cash register in heat?"

You think I'm kidding? They now have a speed line. It's for seven items or $48—whichever is less.

When supermarket checkers finish lunch, they don't call it "going back to work." It's more like "returning to the scene of the crime"!

I'd like to dedicate this next number to supermarket prices: "Off We Go into the Wild Blue Yonder."

Now I know why supermarkets call them sales. A sail is something that's full of wind.

I go back a long time. I can remember supermarkets when, if you picked up an item, the price tags weren't a multiple choice.

It always upsets me to go into a supermarket and see three different prices on a single item. I mean, price increases should be for the needy—not the greedy.

SWIMMING

I've never been attacked by a shark but experts say there are certain telltale little signs that indicate when a shark is about to bite. For instance, if it swims up and begins to squeeze lemon on your leg—watch out!

I'm always amazed at girls who go to the beach and put on all that oil and lotion and grease. You're never quite sure if they're trying to turn your head or your stomach.

Have you ever tried to get romantic with a girl who's covered with oil? It's like opportunity. It keeps slipping through your fingers!

TANS

My wife is crazy about the sun. She spends the whole summer trying to get a deep brown luxurious tan. She says it's sexy— and it is, if you're that way about briefcases!

People are always trying to improve on nature. My wife insisted that I use that aluminum shield that reflects the sun up into your face. And it really did. You're looking at the first man in history who was ever treated for a sunburned sinus!

The first thing a girl learns at the beach is, fellas with deep, rich, golden tans—are unemployed.

TAXES

The only people who don't mind getting flu shots are taxpayers. They're used to getting it in the end!

When we the people of the United States decided to band together to form a more perfect union—I'll bet nobody figured the dues would be so high.

One of the biggest problems in teaching English to foreign visitors is convincing them "damn" and "taxes" are two separate words.

I don't wanna say anything about taxes—but remember the good old days when bankruptcy was do-it-yourself?

The income tax is great for anyone who's given up smoking, because it gives your hands something to do—like shake!

I got my tax bill.
I really am awed.
I earned more money—
Than I can afford!

Did you read about that call girl who owes $100,000 in back taxes? You can imagine what her front owes!

An audit is a tax debate.

TEACHERS

Show me a woman who can rise above her troubles and I'll show you a teacher who wears five-inch heels.

Teachers really need more money just to do their job. Do you realize what a gun, a whip and a chair cost these days?

Personally, I'm for giving teachers anything they want. I mean, I *have* to deal with my kids—they don't. . . . I think the first thing any schoolteacher studies is Masochism 101.

This will go down in history as the era when kids stopped bringing an apple to the teacher and started bringing something she can really use—a box of Excedrin.

TEENAGERS

I don't have to do this for a living, you know. I could always go back to my old job, explaining what clothes hangers are to teenagers.

Seventeen is that wonderful age when a girl is half child and half woman. I've got a daughter who's seventeen and her biggest problem at parties is what wine goes with Twinkies?

My teenager isn't really used to any hard labor. He once got a hernia singing a work song.

I just heard a frightening thing. Two teenagers were studying the instructions on a bottle of floor wax and one read, "It says to apply evenly with a damp mop—whatever that is."

People are always criticizing teenagers but, believe me, there are a lot of kids who aren't making love in drive-in movies. The woods are full of them!

Have you heard the language that teenagers use these days? I heard two parents talking and the mother said, "Somebody made an obscene phone call to our daughter last night." And the father said, "How?"

I was always interested in romance. When I was ten, I played house with the girl next door. When I was thirteen, I played house with the girl next door. When I was sixteen, I played dude ranch with the girl next door. That's like house only there's a little more horsing around.

I'll say one thing for my teenager: he always knows where his head is at. So do I. Until noon, it's on a pillow.

There's a brand-new scent that's driving teenagers out of their minds. They've never experienced anything like it. It's called "Clean!"

TELEPHONES

After sleeping for twenty years, Rip Van Winkle woke up to a whole new generation, a brand-new country, and 73,000 messages at his answering service.

They just gave the phone company another increase. I don't know how this will affect the rates but I just saw a pay phone that takes singles.

The phone company had better be careful about raising the rates. There are very few conversations worth the money now.

They say children bring warmth into a home and I believe it. I get hot every time I see the phone bill!

Ma Bell really keeps up with the times. Do you know they now have a phone with a cord five miles long? It's for kids who want to run away from their parents but not their friends.

Last night I called my son in, showed him an $83 phone bill, and said, "Tell me again how you have difficulty in communicating."

You can't believe how much time kids spend talking to each other. I have one son we call the Phone Ranger!

My wife loves to worry. If she answers the phone and there's complete silence on the other end, she figures it's an obscene phone call from Marcel Marceau.

I'll say this for those 1914 wall phones. At least you quit talking when your feet got tired. . . . What you're resting on now has a lot more endurance.

I'll tell you how nearsighted I am. Yesterday I tried to dial a pencil sharpener!

TELEVISION

An executive we know didn't realize how much overtime he was putting in until his baby daughter said her first word: "Daddy!" What she said it to was the TV set.

There's nothing unusual about our TV set. It has three kids in front and two installments behind.

I get so confused. Like, every time I hear the words "garbage strike"—I think people have stopped watching television.

Have you seen the new TV shows? They're all alike. I don't know if they were filmed or Xeroxed.

This new TV season has been so dull, I happen to know that

three important groups are worried about the consequences—the networks, the critics and Planned Parenthood.

One TV series stopped so fast the entire cast got whiplash!

Cultural TV programs are the ones that get a grant from an oil company and a grunt from your kids.

The TV scene is one that has developed without a taint. But tell me, why do they call them specials, when most of them simply ain't?

I looked up tonight's TV programs in the newspaper. Under BEST BET they listed the OFF button.

They say interest rates are dropping. I know mine are. Every time I watch the Late Movie I fall asleep.

This may seem hard to believe, but I saw a movie on TV that was so old, the girl said, "No!"

I hate to look at the credits on a bad TV show. It's like reading the passenger list on the *Titanic*.

Last night I watched a very thought-provoking TV show. The thought it provoked was: Why am I watching this show?

Overkill is a Sominex commercial on one of the new TV shows.

Sometimes the most imaginative thing on TV is the repairman's bill.

One of the worst things you can run into is a TV repairman who charges $35 an hour and has two great weaknesses—beer and kidneys.

This show is so daring, you can only watch it on a TV set that's twenty-one years or older.

There is no doubt in my mind that television causes violence.

Last night I was trying to watch a baseball game, and I told my kid if he interrupted me one more time with a question about his homework he was gonna get it!

I heard a wild thing on a game show last night. The emcee asked a contestant: "Why did George Washington stand up in the boat crossing the Delaware? But first, this message from Preparation H."

TELEVISION NEWS

The human race is paying its dues.
If you don't believe it, tune in the news!

TV news broadcasts are turning a lot of us into Quakers. I shake every time I hear one.

I'm an optimist. I watch the Five O'Clock News, the Six O'Clock News, and the Seven O'Clock News. I keep hoping it'll get better.

Hear no evil, see no evil, and speak no evil—and you'll never get to be the anchor man on the Seven O'Clock News.

If there's no divine plan for this world, how come just enough happens each day to fill the Seven O'Clock News?

TENNIS

I lost interest in tennis when I found out "Fifteen–Love" wasn't an orgy.

My brother-in-law lost interest in tennis when he found out that "serve" had nothing to do with food.

I can understand why tennis is so popular these days. You ever try to leap over a volleyball net?

Tennis is a fascinating game, particularly if you're middle-aged. If there was no such thing as tennis, cardiologists would have had to invent it.

To be a good tennis player, you have to be thin. Really thin. Like, not only can you jump over the net, but through it too!

One of the great medical problems today is tennis elbow. It comes from watching tennis on television with your elbow on a bar.

THANKSGIVING

It's Thanksgiving. Let's all microfilm our troubles and Xerox our blessings.

The Pilgrims didn't have an easy time of it. Can you imagine eating a meal of turkey, stuffing, gravy, cranberries, corn, cider, squash, rolls, turnips, pumpkin pie, apple pie, mince pie and fruit—when Alka-Seltzer was still three hundred years away?

The Pilgrims were the people who had those guns with the barrel that looked like a lily. They were called "cold tablet" guns. You pulled the trigger and the bullet could go four ways.

If you're ever feeling unloved, unwanted and unnoticed—just imagine how the celery feels at a Thanksgiving dinner.

Thanksgiving dinner is a very time-consuming event. It takes an hour to eat; a day to cook; a week to arrange; and a few months to pay for.

Thanksgiving dinner is the American equivalent to a Chinese dinner. You eat it and a year later you're hungry again.

Restaurants are so crowded on Thanksgiving Day, they make a fortune selling Indian cocktails. Indian cocktails—that's what you drink while you're waiting for your reservation.

This is the month we play Thanksgiving roulette. That's when six different friends invite you to Thanksgiving dinner and one is on Weight Watchers.

We always go to Grandmother's on Thanksgiving Day. She owns a McDonald's.

I always take my family and all the relatives out for Thanksgiving dinner. I figure the wife I save may be my own.

Thanksgiving is when millions of Americans get together to drink, talk, eat and go home again. It's known as the Four Gs —Giggle, Gabble, Gobble and Git!

Every Thanksgiving we have relatives over, and my wife has come up with a great recipe for roasting the turkey. You cook it one family argument for each five pounds.

My neighbor has an interesting theory about Thanksgiving. He feels that most families have so many relatives coming over for Thanksgiving dinner, they'll never notice one more. So for the last ten years he's been going into some strange house on Thanksgiving Day and saying he's Uncle Harry. Nine times it worked out well—the tenth time it worked out great. There was another phony claiming she was Aunt Harriet and they put them up for the night.

Inviting your relatives over for Thanksgiving dinner performs a very useful function. It eliminates loneliness, quiet and leftovers.

One year they all burped at the same time and blew out windows in Omaha, Nebraska!

You don't know what fear is until you've invited twenty-five people over for Thanksgiving dinner and your wife is making it from a mix!

I knew we were in trouble this Thanksgiving the minute my wife asked me to carve the Big Mac.

And my wife made a gravy I'll never forget. One quart of vodka, two quarts of rum and three quarts of brandy. I asked her, "Where did you get this recipe?" She said, "From a cookbook." I said, "Who wrote it?" She said, "Betty Crocked!"

I like those turkeys you can just stick in the oven. You know the ones. For two whole months before Thanksgiving Day they're mainlining butter!

We had a very upsetting thing happen at Thanksgiving dinner. One of the guests complained that the turkey was tough. What made it so upsetting, it was our butcher.

I don't want to brag, but we have an oven that can cook our Thanksgiving turkey in three minutes. It's not a microwave oven. It's a two-pound turkey.

We had kind of an exciting Thanksgiving last year. My wife's recipe for stuffing called for a dash of salt—and she used Epsom. If you think the salt had a dash, you should have seen us!

I have to admit, I have a terrible time carving turkey. I'll tell you how bad it is—one year the turkey's family sued for malpractice.

I'm one of those nervous carvers. I shake so much, each year we have an etiquette problem. What wine do you serve with fingers?

And every Thanksgiving I get very suspicious of butchers.

Yesterday I saw one trying to teach a parakeet to say, "Gobble! Gobble! Gobble!"

For Thanksgiving, the Poultry Raisers of America are sending the biggest turkey in the country to the White House. The (OPPOSITION PARTY) claim he's already there.

There's an ongoing historical inaccuracy about that first Thanksgiving. History books tell us the Pilgrims ate wild turkeys. That isn't so. The turkeys weren't wild—until they found out what the Pilgrims had in mind.

I know a farmer who has a foolproof way of getting ready for Thanksgiving. For a week before, all he does is show the turkeys the Seven O'Clock News, the morning headlines, the editorials, *Time* and *Newsweek*—then they go quietly. Some even volunteer.

Feeling down and tired of living?
Then here's a thought for this Thanksgiving:
If you think your future's murky—
Compare it to that of a turkey!

Thanksgiving is when turkeys who fatten up all year go to the chopping block. With humans, it's April 15th.

Thanksgiving turkeys have the same complaint as our receptionist: "All they want is my body!"

I once roasted a turkey and he really took it hard. Kept calling me a no-good baster.

Some people get squeamish about raising their own turkey for Thanksgiving, but not me. One year we bought a live turkey in January. We called him Clarence and all through the year we fed him, took him for walks, played with him. He was just like one of the family. But when it came November there was no nonsense about it. We had him for Thanksgiving dinner. He sat on my right.

We had spaghetti for Thanksgiving dinner. I won't say why we had spaghetti for Thanksgiving dinner but that's the last time I ever buy a turkey that knows karate!

I watched some of those special Thanksgiving shows on TV and I wanna tell you something: all the turkeys weren't in ovens!

And after one of our Thanksgiving dinners everybody likes to sit back and enjoy a good smoke. It's the one coming from the oven!

Now I sit me down to eat.
The food looks great, the setting neat;
And if I overdo it, well, sir—
Would you pass the Bromo Seltzer?

Thanksgiving is when 200,000,000 Americans gorge themselves on turkey dinners—then turn on the TV to watch 22 football players get exercise.

The day after Thanksgiving is when you can go to any garage sale in America and get a good buy on half a turkey.

THEFT

Two drunks came out of a bar and saw someone siphoning gas out of their car. One drunk nudged the other and said, "Man, I hope I never get that thirsty!"

Last night our house was broken into and robbed, but it's just wonderful the detailed record the police keep on these things. We were the thirty-fourth ditto mark from the top.

I've been robbed three times in the last year and I've had it. The next time I'm robbed, I'm gonna call the cops. You should hear what I'm gonna call the cops!

One year we went away on vacation and burglars broke in and got $150. So the next year I got smart. I left on all the lights and turned on all the radios, plus the two television sets —and burglars didn't get a cent! But the electric company got $489.53!

You can't win. Last week I spent $800 for sound equipment—a tuner, a turntable, six big speakers and a phonograph record of a mean, vicious, snarling police dog. And every time I go out I put on this record in the empty apartment. Well, what can I tell you? Last night I'm cleaned out—but the cops caught the burglar. It was Novelty Night. . . . And I said to the burglar, "You really must have courage. Weren't you put off by all that snarling and growling and barking inside?" He said, "Eh?" (CUPPING YOUR HAND BEHIND YOUR EAR)

You know what's so discouraging about city life? I have three locks, two bolts and a chain on my door—and it takes me longer to get *out* than burglars to get in!

It's ridiculous. I have so many keys on my keyring, if I ever went on "What's My Line?" they'd guess right away who I was—the warden at Sing Sing!

TOYS

Nowadays it's amazing the things they have for kids—like ten-speed bikes. Ten-speed! When I was a kid we had three-speed bikes—fast, slow and broken!

They used to be guaranteed for a lifetime. Not your lifetime— *its!*

I never realized how prophetic those electric trains we had years ago really were. But if you remember, all of the passenger cars were empty.

My wife pampers our kid. She really does. I mean, who else
has an air-conditioned skateboard?

TRAVEL

I'm always amazed at all the people who take ego trips and
carry so little luggage.

Traveling is no problem if you remember one thing: always
wear checked pants. Travelers Checked pants.

The only time most people look like their passport photos is
during a hijacking.

I just got back from one of those tours that take you to six
countries in seven days. It's the nearest thing I know to making love in a revolving door.

We spent three entire hours in Rome. We were in and out of
the Vatican so fast, God said, "What was that?"

I don't want to brag but I did see the Loch Ness monster. It
was a tourist guide who charged me ten dollars to see the
Loch Ness monster.

There's only one trouble with those places that feature sand,
sun and surf. You come back burned, bushed and broke.

Each year I try to take my vacation in some friendly country
and this year we really had a fantastic three weeks. We spent
it in a travel agency trying to find a friendly country.

"A journey of a thousand miles begins with a single step." It's
the one you take when you go back to see if you really did
turn off all the lights.

I always travel by bus. I have nothing against planes—but I've
never heard of a bus running out of gas and falling up!

T-SHIRTS

Can you imagine if Voltaire were alive today? "I disapprove of your T-shirt, but I will defend to the death your right to wear it!"

I can remember when T-shirts were underwear. Now they're more like bumper stickers for humans.

What do you say to a kid who's wearing a T-shirt with a message against pollution—and it's stained?

Last week my teenager came up with the most profound philosophical concept this world has ever known—but he had to discard it. Wouldn't fit on a T-shirt.

UNEMPLOYMENT

Something has got to be done about unemployment. Do you realize that _____% of the American labor force are without jobs? I heard it this morning on my Sony TV set.

He isn't lazy. It's just that there isn't too much demand for his line of work. He's a marriage counselor to the Pope.

A former museum curator was explaining to the clerk at the unemployment office how he lost his job. He said, "Everything was going fine until they got that million-dollar vase and they asked me to identify the name H. T. Rowloow on the bottom." The clerk said, "And you couldn't." The curator said, "No, I could. It was Woolworth spelled backwards."

You know what bothers me most about being unemployed? Taking those coffee breaks on your own time!

Everybody's economizing. Remember Snow White? She just laid off three dwarfs!

VACATIONS

I had a vacation I'll never forget. The charge slips keep reminding me.

If you're traveling with two young kids in the back seat, it isn't really a vacation. It's World War III with coloring books.

Have you ever seen the back seat of a car after two kids have spent three weeks in it? Crayola Canyon! . . . Everything is covered with wax. Looks like Madame Tussaud's during a heat wave!

It's amazing. I didn't think anybody could get into that much trouble in a back seat and still have their clothes on!

And this vacation taught me one thing about being in a car with one wife, two kids and a dog. Stop and go has nothing to do with the traffic!

I had a marvelous rest and why not? I was always parked in front of a room devoted to it.

Whenever we start a vacation, it's the same thing. We get up at six o'clock in the morning to get an early start. First we eat breakfast; then we pack; then we notify the neighbors and Police Department; then we stop the milk, mail and newspaper deliveries; then we arrange for a kid to mow the lawn and water the garden; then we take the dog to the kennel; then the kids say good-by to their friends; then we set the lights that go on automatically, activate the burglar alarm system, lock all the doors and windows—and after all this is finally done, you know what we do? We go to bed because I hate night driving!

My wife is very good about vacations. Each year she says, "We'll go anywhere you'd like." Then she hands me a list of places I'd like.

We spent our vacation getting a suntan and breathing in the clean salt air. It was easy. We sat on our patio and ate herring.

I don't want to shock anybody, but my wife and I spent last night sleeping with our neighbors. We were watching the slides from their vacation.

Did you ever get the feeling that vacations were thought up by Eastman Kodak?

The greatest vacation cottage is one that visits twelve and sleeps two.

VALENTINE'S DAY

My wife is the soft, romantic, sloppily sentimental type. You can tell that by the Valentine's Day present she gave me—denture cleaner!

Be careful what you do on Valentine's Day. A five-pound box of chocolates has put an end to many a loved one.

I never knew why my wife had a weight problem until I gave her a heart-shaped box of chocolates on February 14th—and all day long she just sat there, eating her heart out.

I know we're living in a changing world but I still get shook up when I see three people buying Valentine cards—two kids and a priest.

The stores are all stocked for February 14th. I saw one Valentine card that says: I LOVE YOU TERRIBLY. If you buy it they try to sell you a sex manual too.

Sometimes I wish I had a name like Phantasmagoria Rumpelstiltskin. By the time a girl says, "Phantasmagoria Rumpelstiltskin—no!"—it's too late!

VOTING

What upsets me on Election Day are the people who only need ten seconds to vote but who need two minutes to find their way out of the booth!

You can always tell the responsible prepared voters on Election Day. They're the ones who flipped the coin at home.

Voting booths consist of poles and curtains, which is very fair. When the polls went to _____, it was curtains for _____

I can't understand people who want to register guns. I mean, who would a gun vote for?

WALL STREET

I saw a very disturbing sign on Wall Street. It said: THE BUCK DROPS HERE!

Wall Street has gone stock raving mad!

You can always tell when prosperity has come back to Wall Street. You look on a window ledge and see three more pigeons than brokers.

You remember Wall Street—the Getting Ghetto.

Do you ever get the feeling that somewhere in a little cubicle on Wall Street there's a telegraph operator valiantly tapping out a message? "S.O.S.! S.O.S.! Save Our Stocks!"

Wall Street is suffering from a terrible air pollution problem. It's from all those profits going up in smoke.

I think they're getting a little desperate down on Wall Street.

They're beginning to pull the Dow Jones components into a circle.

There's a coffee shop in the Wall Street area serving a Stock Market Breakfast: scrambled nest eggs.

But Wall Street always tries to put a good face on whatever happens. For instance, the elevators at the stock exchange don't say UP and DOWN. They say UP and CORRECTION.

WEATHER

I love those recorded weather reports. One time I called up and it went something like this: "The 9:00 A.M. temperature is 20 degrees below zero. The forecast for today is hurricanes with winds up to 140 miles an hour. Three feet of flooding is forecast for downtown with 25 inches of snow in the suburbs. Have a nice day!"

I have an idea that's going to increase the accuracy of the Weather Bureau 100%. It's called a window!

I'll tell you what kind of a Weather Bureau we have. Remember when Noah got on the ark? Well, they predicted "Slightly cloudy."

I used to live in Florida but I got out because of the hurricanes. I'll never forget when that last hurricane hit. I looked up at the clock and the little hand was on eight and the big hand was on Georgia.

Yes, we walked through the storm with our heads held high! And you know what we got? Stiff necks and soggy shoes!

The weather is so dry in this town, it's the first time I ever saw anybody baptized with Dr. Pepper.

Talk about lucky breaks. All over the country people are praying for hot air—and Congress is starting up again!

Everybody's freezing. In San Francisco I saw a topless waitress wearing ear muffs—two pair!

WIFE

Socialism is when the state owns everything. Capitalism is when your wife does.

My wife has a wonderful way to make a long story short. She interrupts.

I have a lot of problems. My wife talks to the plants. She talks to the parakeet. She talks to the goldfish. She talks to the dog. *Me* she leaves notes in the refrigerator!

My wife talks to her plants three hours every day. I once asked a geranium, "How do you stand it?" It said, "Who listens?"

I think my wife has the Hong Kong flu. That's when you get up in the middle of the night and you don't cough—you iron shirts!

I think my wife is getting a little hard of hearing. Yesterday the oil tank in our basement exploded, and she said, "Gesundheit!"

I don't really think of her as my wife. She's more like my co-star in twenty years of home movies.

I'm getting a little suspicious of my wife. Last week she got three obscene phone calls—collect!

It's ridiculous. She's listened to more heavy breathing than the telephone operator at Weight Watchers!

I got up this morning, went out to the living room, and we're either going on vacation or moving. My wife does the same amount of packing for each.

It's amazing. One time she packed four dresses, five pants suits, six sports outfits, and seven formal gowns. What makes it so amazing, we were going to a nudist camp.

My business went bankrupt, but my faithful wife Gertrude has stuck by me. I lost all our savings in the stock market, but my faithful wife Gertrude has stuck by me. The bank foreclosed the mortgage on our house, but my faithful wife Gertrude has stuck by me. And now the finance company has repossessed her new mink coat, but my faithful wife Gertrude has stuck by me. Isn't that right, Gertrude? Gertrude?

I don't want to brag about my wife but she has something that'll knock your eye out—hair curlers.

My wife has two passions in life—soap operas and eating. We have the only refrigerator in town, when you open it, a little TV set goes on.

My wife has never worried about money. You know how some women wash dishes? She has them dry-cleaned!

I never realized how strong my wife is until she planted 40 tulip bulbs—in the Astroturf.

Every time we have an argument, my wife always brings up my past misdeeds. She has a memory like a shiv!

I'm beginning to wonder about my wife. When it's freezing and hailing and sleeting and snowing, she won't let me go out unless I have something that's heavy—like a cold.

I may have to give my wife a loyalty test. Last night I got home from giving a speech and she said, "How did you do?" I said, "I brought down the house." She said, "So do termites."

He just wishes his wife hadn't said she's given him the best years of her life. Now he's as discouraged as she is.

I have an agreement with my wife. She doesn't compare the men in *Playgirl* to me—and I don't compare the meals in *Family Circle* to hers.

WINTER

Winter is when fathers all over America shovel paths to the sidewalk so their teenagers can get out to make money, shoveling paths out to sidewalks.

January is when you pay a kid $5.00 to shovel the snow out of your driveway, so you can go to the Y for some exercise.

Here it is January again. When the air conditioning repairman you called in July shows up!

January is when you order the flower seeds you plant in April and wonder what happened to in August.

And January is when the President goes on TV to say how things are looking up in the war on inflation—and you realize it's a rerun.

Don't you just hate these cold winter mornings, when your car won't start running and your nose won't stop?

February is the Mickey Rooney of months.

If you need a bit of glow and a dash of warmth to help you through this difficult winter, get out a spring seed catalog—and throw it on the fire.

WOMEN'S LIB

Frankly, I'm amazed there are so many Avon ladies. Nowadays, where do you find a woman who'll take orders?

I'm reading a book about the most intense emotional conflict a person has ever experienced. It's the story of a member of Women's Lib who just received from her boy friend a diamond-studded, ruby-encrusted, solid gold slave bracelet.

I don't care how secure a man is, he's got to feel a little uneasy going to a Women's Lib wienie roast.

Women's Liberation has really made it in our neighborhood. Last night I was held up by a gunperson.

Women's Liberation has a real struggle on their hands. Do you realize how far back male vanity goes? All the way to the Garden of Eden when Adam said, "I don't know if this fig leaf is going to be large enough."

The role of women is really changing. There's a little old lady next door who spends all her time reading *The Joy of Sex* and knitting a whip.

WORK

Kids today don't recognize opportunity because it comes disguised as work.

Some people are just born for their work—like an exterminator with flat feet!

I keep telling my wife I couldn't live without her. And I couldn't. She's the one who's working!

WORLD CONDITIONS

Americans are the greatest grain producers in the world. We're just fantastic in the sack!

The way the rest of the world is acting, I'm glad we didn't bite the bullet. We may need every one we can get.

Whatever happened to the good old days when the only worry we had overseas was whether to drink the water?

Thanks to nuclear bombs and intercontinental ballistic missiles, you don't ever have to worry about waking up and hearing that war has been declared. If you wake up, it hasn't.

A cease-fire is when trigger mortis sets in.

A TOAST: To the machines of war wherever they are—may they rust in peace!

Personally, I'm used to wars over territory. I've got a five-room house and six kids.

I just bought one of those pens that are guaranteed for life—providing you live in Belfast.

St. Patrick's Day is when Irishmen thousands and thousands of miles from Ireland get together and celebrate—that they're thousands and thousands of miles from Ireland.

The Arabs want to blend their way of life with Western technology and they're already starting to do it. At this very moment in downtown Saudi Arabia, they're putting up the world's tallest structure—a 155-story tent!

Speed reading is very popular in South American countries. It's the only way you can catch the name of the current President.

I wrote this mournful little verse
To make a point, however terse.

If worldly woes get any worse—
A pleasure car will be a hearse!

I'll tell you what kind of a world we're living in. This is the first Thanksgiving I ever saw turkeys volunteer.

We seem to be living in a world that's rich in questions and poor in answers.

What this world really needs is a placebo that works!

On behalf of all the peoples of the world, I'd like to say one thing: "This just hasn't been our century!"

Pessimists never had it so good!

We're living in an era of fast-changing terminology. For instance, we now have a new name for the leader of our church —the chairparson.

X-RATED MOVIES

An X-rated movie is an underdeveloped plot with an over-developed cast.

You have to give Karl Marx credit for being farsighted. Do you realize that, sixty years before X-rated movies, he said, "Workers of the world, unite!"

It bothers me when educators refer to it as "formal sex education." It always sounds like they're watching X-rated movies in a tuxedo.

A senior citizen went up to the box office and the cashier said, "This movie is rated X. Do you know what that stands for?" He said, "I sure do. If you're my age—Xasperating!"

You could tell the audience enjoyed it. Talk about heavy breathing. It sounded like the track team at Sun City.

Every time I get an attack of asthma I go to an X-rated movie. It's a shame to waste all that heavy breathing.

And sometimes it isn't a good idea taking your wife to a movie like this. After it was over, she leaned over and called me "Don Juan." I said, "Because I'm such a great lover?" She said, "No. Because Juan and you're Don!"

Three salesmen from (YOUR TOWN) met by chance at a convention in New York City. One said he had never been to New York City before and he was planning to take a sightseeing bus to all the famous sights. The second salesman said he was an art buff and planned to visit the Metropolitan Museum of Art, the Museum of Modern Art and the Frick Collection. The third salesman said he planned to attend services at some of the great religious institutions such as St. Patrick's Cathedral and the Cathedral of St. John the Divine. And just by chance the very next day these three salesmen met again—in an X-rated movie.

I come from a town that's so small, they can't afford X-rated movies. Once a week someone just volunteers to leave their shade up.

ONE PICTURE IS WORTH A THOUSAND WORDS. Only if it's X-rated.

I just saw my first X-rated Western. Even the wagons weren't covered.

In 1775 we had Minute Men. Today we still have Minute Men. It's anyone who goes out to the candy stand during an X-rated movie.

Have you noticed how X-rated movies and Westerns have one thing in common? The heroes never have to stop to reload.

My doctor won't let me see X-rated movies for medical reasons. He says if you don't blink your eyes every ten seconds you go blind.

Things are so bad, I like to go to X-rated movies. It's a pleasure to see someone making out.

I'm not a big fan of X-rated movies. I liked things better when dogs shed and people didn't.